Physical Characteristics of the Bracco Italiano
(from the Fédération Cynologique Internationale)

Body: *Topline*—The upper profile of the back is made up of two lines: one, almost straight, slopes from the withers to the 11th dorsal vertebra; the other is slightly arched, joining with the line of the rump. *Withers*—Well defined, with the points of the shoulder blades well separated. *Loin*—Wide lumbar region, muscled, short and slightly convex. *Rump*—Long (about one-third of the height at the withers), broad and well muscled. *Chest*—Broad, deep and well down to level of elbows, without forming a heel, with well sprung ribs, particularly in their lower part, and sloping. *Underline*—Lower profile almost horizontal in its rib cage part, rising slightly in its abdominal part.

Tail: Thick at the base, straight, with a slight tendency to taper, hair short. Should be docked at 15–25 cm from the root.

Hindquarters: Thigh long, parallel, muscular, with a rear edge almost straight; strong limbs; hocks wide, metatarsals relatively short and lean. The feet, with all the characteristics of the front feet, have dewclaws.

Coat: Short, dense and glossy, fine and shorter on the head, the ears, front part of the legs and feet.

Size and Weight: Height at the withers between 55–67 cm. Preferred size for males: 58–67 cm; preferred size for females: 55–62 cm. Weight between 25 and 40 kg, depending on height.

Color: White; white with marking of varied size of an orange or more or less dark amber color, white with more or less large chestnut marking; white with pale orange (speckled); white mottled with chestnut (roan-chestnut).

Bracco Italiano

By Juliette Cunliffe

9   History of the Bracco Italiano

Known in its homeland since the Middle Ages, the Bracco Italiano has been a prized hunting companion of Italian nobility. Learn about the unique way that the breed works, plus how fanciers have preserved the abilities throughout the generations. Follow the Bracco as it begins to capture attention outside Italy.

17   Characteristics of the Bracco Italiano

A working dog by nature, the Bracco Italiano also possesses many traits that make him a wonderful companion and family dog for the right owners. Explore the breed's personality, physical characteristics and health concerns to help you decide if this is the dog for you.

26   Breed Standard for the Bracco Italiano

Learn the requirements of a well-bred Bracco Italiano by studying the descriptions of the breed as set forth by the Fédération Cynologique Internationale. Both show dogs and pets must possess key characteristics as outlined in the standard.

36   Your Puppy Bracco Italiano

Be advised about choosing a reputable breeder and selecting a healthy, typical puppy. Understand the responsibilities of ownership, including home preparation, acclimatization, the vet and prevention of common puppy problems.

59   Everyday Care of Your Bracco Italiano

Enter into a sensible discussion of dietary and feeding considerations, exercise, grooming, traveling and identification of your dog. This chapter discusses Bracco Italiano care for all stages of development.

80   Training Your Bracco Italiano

By Charlotte Schwartz
Be informed about the importance of training your Bracco Italiano from the basics of housebreaking and understanding the development of a young dog to executing obedience commands (sit, stay, down, etc.).

Contents

Health Care of Your Bracco Italiano — 105

Discover how to select a qualified vet and care for your dog at all stages of life. Topics include vaccinations, skin problems, dealing with external and internal parasites and common medical and behavioral conditions.

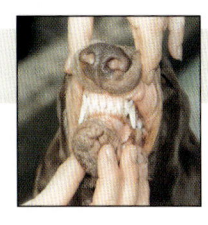

Your Senior Bracco Italiano — 137

Consider the care of your senior Bracco Italiano, including the proper diet for a senior. Recognize the signs of an aging dog, both behavioral and medical; implement a special-care program with your vet and become comfortable with making the final decisions and arrangements for your senior Bracco Italiano.

Showing Your Bracco Italiano — 141

Enter the world of showing dogs. Learn about the different types of shows and the making up of a champion. Go beyond the conformation ring to find out about agility and obedience trials, and other performance events.

Behavior of Your Bracco Italiano — 146

Learn to recognize and handle behavioral problems that may arise with your Bracco Italiano. Topics discussed include separation anxiety, aggression, barking, chewing, digging, begging, jumping up, etc.

Index 156

KENNEL CLUB BOOKS: BRACCO ITALIANO
ISBN: 1-59378-372-8

Copyright © 2003 Kennel Club Books, Inc.
308 Main Street, Allenhurst, NJ 07711 USA
Cover Design Patented: US 6,435,559 B2 • Printed in South Korea

All rights reserved. No part of this book may be reproduced in any form, by photostat, scanner, microfilm, xerography or any other means, or incorporated into any information retrieval system, electronic or mechanical, without the written permission of the copyright owner.

Photographs by Alice van Kempen,
with additional photos by:
Norvia Behling, T.J. Calhoun, Carolina Biological Supply, Juliette Cunliffe, Doskocil, Isabelle Français, James Hayden-Yoav, James R. Hayden, RBP, Carol Ann Johnson, Bill Jonas, Dwight R. Kuhn, Dr. Dennis Kunkel, Mikki Pet Products, Phototake, Jean Claude Revy and Dr. Andrew Spielman.

Illustrations by Patricia Peters.

8 BRACCO ITALIANO

A spectacular sight in action, the Bracco Italiano is a native Italian hunting breed that is prized for its well-rounded abilities in all aspects of the field.

HISTORY OF THE
BRACCO ITALIANO

The Bracco Italiano is the Italian Pointer, and one of only two native Italian gundog breeds, both of which are known as Hunt, Point and Retrieve dogs, familiarly known as HPR. The other such breed is the Italian Spinone, and both are held in high esteem in their country of origin.

The Bracco is an elegant and athletic dog, a classic and ancient pointer whose origins, many say, can be traced back to the fourth and fifth centuries BC. There are various theories about the breed's origin, but it appears most likely that it developed from the Molossus and the Egyptian Hound, and that it is an antecedent of many modern sporting dogs today.

In Italy, the Bracco is accepted as having been a distinct breed since the Middle Ages. During the Renaissance period, the breed became widespread, being held in especially high regard by the nobility. This was due to the fact that hunting feathered game was an exclusive sport of Italy's aristocracy. The Gonzaga and Medici families bred the Bracco Italiano, and dogs from their kennels were eagerly sought by nobility and those of royal rank.

There are frescoes from the 14th century that depict the breed's existence at that time. It is believed that the white and orange variety originated in Piedmont, with the white and chestnut dog hailing from Lombardy. The type from Piedmont was generally lighter in construction than the other and, because of its lighter build, was better suited for work in the mountains. Indeed, the two types were at one time referred to as the "Piedmontese Pointer" and the "Lombard Pointer," but, as time passed, breeders amalgamated the two types so that now the breed is more uniform in size.

Some people, however, believe that the Bracco Italiano came into being only as recently as the 17th century, arising from hound and gundog breeds. People of this belief rightly point out that the Bracco has the head of a hound and the body of a gundog, and they also consider the Bracco's temperament to be a mixture of the two.

BRED TO WORK, AND KEPT THAT WAY

In Italy, the breed was developed specifically to work. The Bracco's role was to drive game into the hunters' nets. Only with the invention of the gun did the breed's role change to that of HPR, and the breed developed further to accommodate the needs of the hunters.

At the close of the 19th and beginning of the 20th centuries, the Bracco Italiano almost disappeared into oblivion. However, thanks to the enthusiastic Italian breeder, Ferdinando Delor de Ferrabouc (1838–1913), the breed was saved from extinction and has survived until this day. Ferdinando Delor not only was a fancier of the breed but also was a hunter, show judge and field-trial judge. Furthermore, he served as editor of specialized magazines, including that of the Italian Kennel Club, of which he was an important founder. We owe the very first drafts of the standard for the Bracco Italiano to this man.

Particularly involved with the Bracco, Spinone and Pointer breeds, Ferdinando Delor was highly prominent in dogs in the years leading up to and following the turn of the 20th century. In his memory, a trophy is still awarded for pointing dogs; competition for this award is among the best Italian, English and other European dogs.

In Italy, the definitive breed standard for the Bracco Italiano was issued by the Italian Kennel Club (ENCI) on February 19, 1949, and it should be noted that this standard allows for both the heavier and lighter types. In November of that same year, the

History 11

The Segugio Italiano is another Italian hunting hound. Inset: Head study of the Segugio.

BRACCO ITALIANO

Società Amatori Bracco Italiano (SABI) was founded. To this day, SABI has striven to maintain the high quality of the breed, maintaining good health and type without losing any of the Bracco's instinctive hunting ability. SABI is now essentially the custodian of the Bracco Italiano in Italy and has worked extremely hard to revive this magnificent dog, which has deservedly grown stronger in popularity from year to year.

THE BRACCO ITALIANO AT WORK

The Bracco Italiano is not only a stylish hunter but also an enthusiastic one with a splendid nose. This is a breed that will hold a point and retrieve keenly. Although originally used without the gun, by means of allowing the falconers to fly their hawks or the hunters to deploy their nets before flushing the quarry, they are now used to hunt, point and retrieve. Retrieving was something the

The Italian hound known as the Spinone shares the distinction, along with the Bracco, of being one of two native Italian HPR breeds.

Bracco had not done hitherto.

In 1937, a Working Standard was drawn up in Italy, this known as "The Pastrone Standard." It was very specific in its description of how the breed was to work, with a long, brisk trot, tolerating a brief period of galloping when returning on ground already inspected or when the dog was strangely excited. The standard specified that the gait was lively and almost always in a straight line for 100 meters (330 feet) or more. Preoccupation with the scent was of the utmost importance, requiring a complex mental process.

The hunt was extremely diligent. The stub of the Bracco's tail, held upright, was in joyful, almost continuous, transversal motion. Upon detecting a scent, the dog would gradually slow down and return, with great prudence, to the presumed origin, his head held high, his ears cocked and his slightly lowered tail held stiffly. If the scent were leading him closer to the game, he would slow down even more, often feeling the ground with his paw before placing it on the ground, seemingly afraid to make any noise. When motionless, his tail was still, raised slightly, and the dog in horizontal poise.

This Working Standard builds a vivid word-picture when it says, "The combined comportment of the dog is noble, imposing, alert but calm, erect and slightly forward balanced. The neckline is a little raised and the head erect with the nose decisively towards the ground (approx. 30° from the horizontal)." If, during the search, the dog crossed a scent that made him instantly certain of the game's presence, he would slow and take up a general posture, similar to that when stationary, but with his neckline a little more pronounced and his tail held a little lower.

SLOW BUT STEADY SPREAD
Although numerically strongest in its homeland, Italy, the Bracco is now known in several different countries throughout the world, albeit often still in small numbers. This elegant, versatile breed is working its way into the hearts of many who want a good-looking companion that is highly capable of work.

An early illustration of the Bracco Italiano.

When the Bracco later sensed that he was suddenly upon the game, he would stop immediately, staying more often than not upright, his limbs a little flexed and his head turned down to the ground, or lowered, toward the game. In exceptional cases, the dog at this stage would squat in a contorted pose.

Should the game attempt to escape, the Bracco would guide the game to the wind, proceeding with caution to avoid dry branches or noisy leaves, while always maintaining a motionless tension. Thus the dog would repeat the tracking action, prudently but decisively.

When the game found itself on especially favored ground, and tried to make its escape, the Bracco became a prudent and tenacious tracker. A Bracco was always to have complete contact with his handler, and the dog's calm and reflective nature was ideal for work in accordance with the conditions encountered.

Indeed, the Bracco works in much the same way today. Individual dogs point in different ways, but they have in common the fact that their heads are unmoving and fixed, and that their feet are rooted to the spot. On point, the Bracco is expected to produce or flush the quarry upon command. The dog, working in a positive manner, thus causes the bird to fly, or the rabbit or hare to bolt. It is important that the dog remains steady so that the hunter is able to take a shot. Then, on command, the Bracco is expected to quickly find the area where the quarry lies and retrieve it to hand without any damage.

THE BRACCO IN THE UNITED STATES

The Bracco Italiano is still virtually unknown in the US, and in North America as a whole, and is still in its formative years of establishment. However, meetings are held for dedicated and genuine enthusiasts, and thanks to careful selection of stock from abroad, the breed is set to thrive.

Although not recognized by the American Kennel Club, the major governing body of dog registration and events in the US, it is accepted by the United Kennel Club, the American Rare Breeds Association and other rare-breed and all-breed registries. The North American Bracco Italiano Club is a parent club dedicated to the breed in North America; the North American Versatility Hunting Dog Association is a hunting organization that recognizes the Bracco and other hunting breeds. So although the breed is waiting to "arrive" in the US, it does have a promising future, and Americans have a wonderful breed to look forward to.

THE BRACCO ITALIANO IN THE UK

Jonathan and Liz Shaw visited a field trial in Italy in 1988, initially to see Italian Spinone. However, at this trial, they first encountered

HOUND RESEMBLANCE
Although the Bracco Italiano is a gundog breed, in appearance it is somewhat hound-like, indeed more so than any other of the gundog breeds. Facially, the Bracco bears a certain resemblance to the Bloodhound or the Basset Hound, but there is no disputing that this is a true gundog!

Interest in the Bracco is spreading throughout Europe, and the breed is especially enjoying growing popularity in the Netherlands. The Bracco pictured here is being exhibited at a Dutch show.

the Bracco Italiano. The breed made such an impression on them that they brought a Bracco named Zerbo into quarantine in Britain in spring of the following year. Since then, a number of Bracchi have been imported to Britain, primarily by the Shaws. England is one of the countries outside Italy in which the breed enjoys the most popularity.

Although the breed had arrived in Britain some nine years earlier, the Bracco Italiano Society was not formed until 1998, receiving full recognition from the English Kennel Club in 2000. Few litters have been bred in the country since the first import, but breeders have tried to ensure that they breed for quality rather than quantity. In doing so, they have built a firm foundation for the further progress of the breed in Britain.

In Britain, this breed is mainly a companion animal but, having said that, a high proportion of Bracchi actively participate in some kind of work, too. It should always be remembered that a Bracco seems at his happiest when carrying out a job of some sort. Work for the breed can take many forms: performing as gundogs, taking part in working tests and trials, tracking, searching and rescuing, serving as aids in falconry or even working as therapy dogs.

The Bracco Italiano is still on the Import Register with England's Kennel Club (KC), thereby not allowing breed-specific competition at KC-regulated shows. At Open and Championship Shows, the Bracco can only compete among other breeds on the Import Register if such classes are scheduled. The breed is not permitted to compete for Best in Show. Nonetheless, Bracco enthusiasts are interested in both show and working aspects.

CHARACTERISTICS OF THE
BRACCO ITALIANO

WHY THE BRACCO ITALIANO?
There can be no disputing the fact that the Bracco Italiano is a handsome dog, and though presently not especially well-known worldwide, his appearance, character and physique endear him to many, whether or not they will eventually become owners of the breed. The Bracco is a soundly constructed sporting dog with a well-developed brain. He is a friendly dog that is eager to please. Thus, although he is a wonderful companion, he also needs ample opportunity to exercise both his brainpower and his powerful body.

It is generally recommended that only people with previous experience in dog ownership should take on a Bracco Italiano, so this is not an ideal selection as a "first" breed. However, the Bracco makes a great companion dog and is therefore suitable as a family dog, provided the dog is given sufficient training and opportunity for exercise. Most Bracchi even seem to take well to the family cat, though calm, sensible discipline and training, and careful introductions, are important for success. It is generally accepted that the Bracco is better suited to a life in the country than

Equally at home in the field or in water, the Bracco is a skilled retriever in all types of environments.

A SENSITIVE BREED
The Bracco Italiano is eager to learn, but training must be gently firm and always consistent. Owners should never forget that a Bracco is a sensitive dog and does not readily accept being chastised.

as a city-dweller. Those who live in cities and take on Bracchi as pets must ensure that they are in a position to provide their dogs with plenty of frequent exercise.

PERSONALITY
The Bracco is certainly fun to live with, and is a loyal breed with an amazingly good memory for people he likes. Owners say that this is indeed no "ordinary" dog, and this is well founded. Firstly, the Bracco is highly intelligent and seems to have a genuine need not only for companionship but also for exercise and brainwork. He truly enjoys the company of his family and is happy to be a lap dog, but it should always be borne in mind that he wants more than just that; he must also be given an opportunity to work. Work in the shooting field is ideal but, if this is not possible, he can turn his hand (or paw!) to other things, provided he thinks he is doing a "job."

The Bracco does not like to be criticized or chastised. To handle and train this breed successfully, owners need to be gentle, but firm, and preferably they should have a calm nature. Should an owner try to treat a Bracco harshly in any way, the dog will simply "switch off," and training sessions will get absolutely nowhere.

Although the Bracco loves to please, it is not by any means unknown for him to "turn a deaf ear" when it suits him to do so, especially when in hunting mode. He can certainly be willful but, in general, he has a serious yet amiable and biddable temperament, and is both docile and gentle. With those he does not know, he is usually friendly, but he is likely to show a little caution.

PHYSICAL CHARACTERISTICS
This is a strong, powerful dog that is both muscular and robust, yet lean. His long, sloping shoulders

Characteristics

are muscular and well-laid-back, in keeping with his long, well-muscled hindquarters, which allow him to move strongly and with drive. This is a true sporting dog, his construction in keeping with his hunting ability. It is important that the Bracco has well-sprung ribs, with a good depth of brisket, and that his back is strong.

The feet of the Bracco are sturdy and oval in shape, the toes slightly extended. While single dewclaws are preferred, double are accepted.

Head and Ears

Set on a powerful neck, the long, angular head of the Bracco is highly distinctive. In general skeletal appearance, coupled with the shape of his ears, he is considered by many to be reminiscent of a hound rather than a gundog. His occiput is pronounced and the zygomatic arch well developed. The stop is slight, and it is important that the nostrils are wide, indicating that they are well opened. The FCI breed standard makes use of the descriptive word "voluminous" in relation to the nose and describes the head as "markedly sculpted."

The supple ears, whose leathers extend to the end of the muzzle, have slightly rounded tips, are set slightly higher than the level of the eyes and hang close to the cheeks. The oval-shaped eyes are intelligent and attentive in expression, and are found in shades of amber. The strong jaw contains a typical scissors bite, but the FCI also accepts a pincer bite, in which the incisors meet edge to edge.

Tail

The FCI breed standard states that the tail should be docked at 15–25 cm from the root; this represents 6–10 inches, thus allowing rather a wide variance. In countries such as Britain, for example, the docking of tails is a controversial issue at present. The British breed standard simply calls for a tail of medium length, strong at base and

ENERGY AND ENTHUSIASM

The Bracco has lots of energy and, if not given sufficient exercise, can be boisterous. This a true gundog that loves to retrieve, and generally he also makes a good and enthusiastic swimmer. The Bracco loves a country life, and will thoroughly enjoy long walks, with free runs in a suitably controlled and enclosed area.

The magnificent head and strong neck of a well-bred Bracco.

Characteristics

slightly tapered, with qualification that it should be carried below horizontal when at rest and slightly raised when in motion.

Size
This is a substantially built dog, but doubtless the breed's history has some bearing on the flexibility in regard to exact specifications. The FCI standard allows for some range in height, with an overall range between 55–67 cm, but states that the preferred size for males is 58–67 cm (22.75–26.5 in), and for bitches 55-62 cm (21.75–24.5 in). It also gives some guidance as to weight, but again this is wide-ranging, from 25 kg (55 lb) to 40 kg (88 lb), depending on the height of the dog.

The FCI standard also gives a description of the proportions of this breed, and this is worthy of quotation: "Length of the body is the same or a little more than the height at the withers. Length of head is equal to four-tenths of the height at the withers, its width, measured at the level of the zygomatic arches, is less than half its length. Skull and muzzle are of equal length."

Movement
The Bracco Italiano has a brisk, short-striding gait that is straight and true. The FCI standard is rather explicit in its description, saying that the Bracco has an extended and fast trot, with powerful impulsion from the hindquarters. When moving, the head is raised, and the nose is held in such a way that, when hunting, the nose is higher than the topline.

Coat and Color
The short, glossy coat is fine and dense, and is actually shorter on the head, ears and front part of

The Bracco's special combination of temperament and unique physical traits makes him ideally suited for his intended purpose.

> **SKIN AND COLOR**
> The FCI standard gives a detailed description of the breed's skin, which is tough but elastic. On the head and throat, inside the elbows and on the lower part of the body, the skin is fine. Visible mucous membranes must be a color that corresponds with the coat, but must never show black spots. The mucous membranes of the mouth are pink, but dogs with the chestnut color sometimes show brown or light chestnut spotting.

the legs and feet. This is a coat that is easy to maintain in good condition, but, of course, as with all breeds, correct feeding will help to develop a healthy coat, and some routine grooming is a must.

The colors can be orange and white, orange roan, chestnut and white or chestnut roan. Roan is a fine mixture of colored hairs alternating with white ones. In the FCI breed standard, what is described as a metallic sheen is appreciated in chestnut roans, and the chestnut should be of a warm shade, described as like that of a "monk's tunic." Again with reference to the FCI standard, a symmetrical facial mask is preferred but the absence of a mask is tolerated.

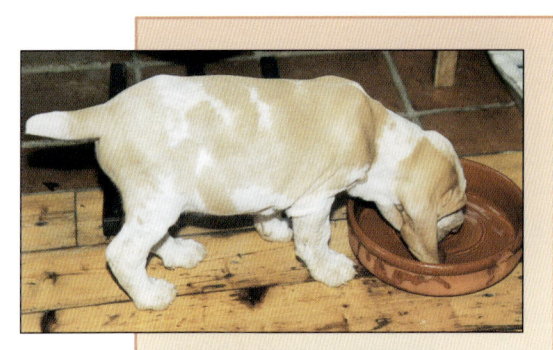

GROWING UP STRONG
In general, the Bracco Italiano is a good eater, but it is essential to remember that a puppy will grow into a large, powerful dog. Hence, in puppyhood especially, a Bracco will require a nutritious diet to ensure healthy formation of bones and joints.

HEALTH CONSIDERATIONS
In general, the Bracco Italiano is a healthy breed, but it is recommended that hips and eyes be tested prior to breeding, to ensure that breeding stock is free of hip dysplasia and hereditary eye disease. However, as with all breeds, some health problems do occur from time to time, and it is in the breed's best interests if new and potential owners know what to look out for. If owners are aware of the problems that can occur, they are undoubtedly in a position to deal with them in the best manner possible.

Hip Dysplasia
Many of the larger breeds, including the Bracco Italiano, are predisposed to hip dysplasia. It is therefore recommended that x-ray testing be carried out under the screening scheme of the country in which you live.

Known often as HD, hip dysplasia is a problem involving the malformation of the ball-and-socket joint at the hip, a developmental condition caused by the interaction of many genes. This results in looseness of the hip joints and, although not always painful, it can cause lameness and can impair typical movement. Although a dog's environment does not actually cause hip dysplasia, this may have some bearing on how unstable the hip joint eventually becomes.

Characteristics 23

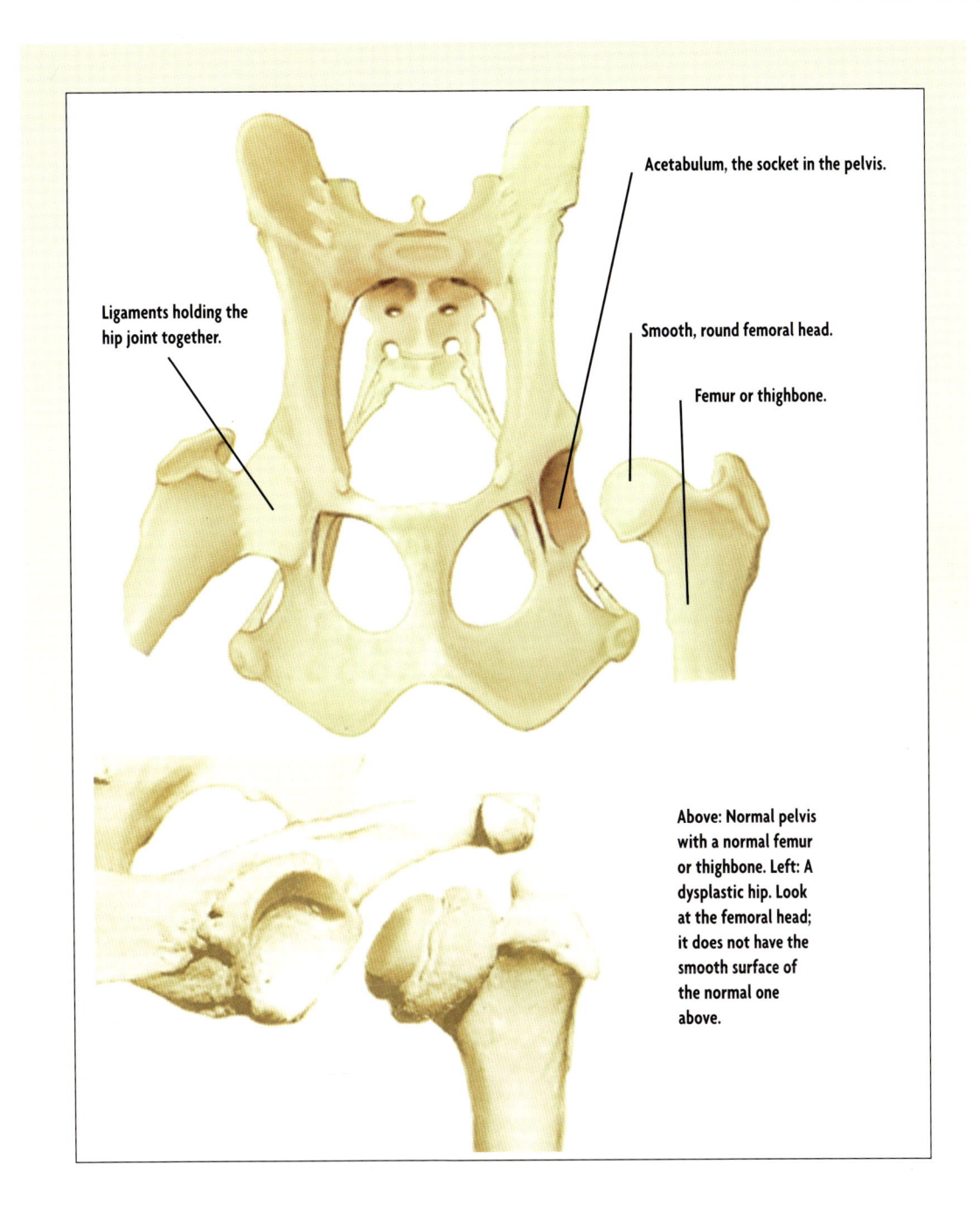

Acetabulum, the socket in the pelvis.

Ligaments holding the hip joint together.

Smooth, round femoral head.

Femur or thighbone.

Above: Normal pelvis with a normal femur or thighbone. Left: A dysplastic hip. Look at the femoral head; it does not have the smooth surface of the normal one above.

Osteoarthritis eventually develops as a result of the instability. Unfortunately there is no cure for hip dysplasia, but there are therapeutic and surgical methods to help the dog live as normal and pain-free a life as possible.

Tests for hip dysplasia are available in most countries throughout the world. Both hips are tested and scored individually; the lower the score, the less the degree of dysplasia. Each testing scheme clearly indicates which scores make a dog ineligible for breeding. Clearly, dogs with scores above the norm should not be incorporated into breeding programs.

Elbow Dysplasia
A form of dysplasia similar to that found in the hip can occur in the elbow. This can affect a dog quite suddenly and can cause lameness, with arthritis usually resulting in the elbow joint. As with hip dysplasia, elbows can be x-rayed to determine the severity, and those dogs that are affected should be eliminated from breeding programs.

Gastric Dilatation/Torsion (Bloat)
Bloat is the more common name for gastric dilatation (rapid enlargement of the stomach), which can result in gastric torsion. This is a twisting of the entrance and exit to the stomach, preventing the escape of gas into the esophagus or duodenum. Bloat is frequently caused by feeding following strenuous exercise; it also can be caused by overeating, especially in young dogs. There is every reason for immediate veterinary treatment, for death can ensue quickly. Ways to prevent bloat in your Bracco as well as how to detect bloat are discussed in detail in the health chapter of this book.

Eyes
It is particularly important to keep a careful check on the cleanliness

---

THE OVERWEIGHT DOG
It is always prudent to keep a careful eye on your Bracco's weight and avoid his becoming overweight, for any dog carrying excess weight tends to be less healthy than one of the correct weight for his breed.

This participant in a recent World Dog Show illustrates a Bracco in top condition.

and condition of your dog's eyes, so as to avoid eye infections' arising. At the first sign of injury, especially if the eye is starting to turn blue in color, urgent veterinary attention is required. Early diagnosis and treatment can often save a dog's sight.

In countries where specialist eye testing is possible, it is advisable to have your Bracco's eyes tested, ideally every year. There are hereditary eye diseases that occur in many breeds, some not until later in life. Therefore, eye testing is imperative to ensure your own dog's health, plus to prevent him from passing on any hereditary problems through breeding. Any dogs affected by or carrying hereditary eye diseases should be excluded from breeding programs.

Heart Problems

Occasionally dogs can suffer from heart problems, particularly as they become more advanced in age. It is therefore sensible to request your vet to check your dog's heart whenever visiting for routine examination or vaccination, though many good vets will do this automatically. Heart checks should certainly be part of your Bracco's regular check-ups.

The very nature of the breed means that a Bracco is always ready to follow his nose.

Heat Exhaustion

Frequently people do not realize how quickly death can result from heat exhaustion. The first sign is heavy panting, and the dog begins to puff or gasp for air. When walking, the dog appears dizzy and tends to weave, subsequently collapsing, with eventual unconsciousness.

At the first sign, the dog should be taken out of the sun and offered water. The body should be doused in water, especially the head and neck, and, if available, ice bags or even a package of frozen vegetables should be placed around head and neck. Because the dog's temperature needs to be lowered urgently, this should be done even before taking your dog to the vet.

TEMPERAMENT DEFINED

The FCI breed standard describes "Behavior and Temperament" of the Bracco Italiano as: "Tough and adapted to all types of hunting, reliable, endowed with an excellent ability to understand, docile and easy to train."

BREED STANDARD FOR THE
BRACCO ITALIANO

INTRODUCTION TO THE BREED STANDARD

All breed standards are designed effectively to paint a picture in words, a picture of the ideal representative of the breed it describes in looks, construction and temperament. These elements combined make a dog that is perfectly suited to perform the breed's original function. Whether or not dogs are used in their intended capacities today, they should still possess the type and ability to do so. A breed standard serves as a blueprint to ensure that a breed will remain consistent throughout the generations, so that the breed will always have the distinct characteristics that make it what it is and that set it apart from all other breeds.

Each reader will almost certainly have a slightly different way of interpreting the words of a breed standard. After all, were everyone to interpret a breed's standard in exactly the same way, there would only be one consistent winner within the breed at any given time!

However, a breed standard undoubtedly helps breeders to produce stock that comes as close as possible to the recognized ideal, and helps judges to know exactly what they are looking for. This enables each judge to make a carefully considered decision when selecting the most typical specimens present to be placed among the winners.

To fully comprehend the intricacies of a breed, reading words alone is never enough. In addition, it is essential for devotees to watch Bracchi being judged at shows whenever the opportunity arises and, if possible, to attend seminars at which the breed is

Head study in profile showing correct type, structure and proportion.

Breed Standard 27

A five-year-old Bracco Italiano, Giacherebbe Dell'Angelo del Summano took top honors at the 2000 World Dog Show, held in Milan, being crowned Best in Show and doing so in his homeland. He is owned by Maeder Isabella.

A Group-One-winning Bracco at an FCI show on the Continent.

discussed. Owners should absorb as much knowledge and understanding as possible about the Bracco Italiano. Additionally, "hands on" experience, providing an opportunity to assess the structure of dogs, is always valuable.

It is important for enthusiasts to read a breed standard over and over again, and, when possible, to couple this with practical experience of assessing a dog. Only in this way can one fully digest the finer points of the breed. There are various areas of any breed standard that are easy to gloss over without much thought, but these fine points are what help to make the breed what it is.

The breed is numerically stronger in mainland Europe than anywhere else in the world at present, with the FCI breed standard (which is that of Italy, the breed's homeland) being the most comprehensive and most widely used around the world. The Bracco Italiano is classified in the FCI's Group 7, Pointing Dogs, Section 1. Its breed standard is number 202, and a translation is presented here.

THE FCI BREED STANDARD FOR THE BRACCO ITALIANO (ITALIAN POINTER)

Brief Historical Summary

This dog of ancient Italian origin used for bird hunting has developed over the ages; from the hunting by nets to hunting with guns. Frescoes from the 14th century are proof of the indisputable timelessness of the Italian Pointer over the centuries, regarding the morphology and aptitudes in hunting as a pointer.

General Appearance

Of strong and harmonious construction, powerful appearance. The preferred subjects are those with lean limbs, well-developed muscles, well-defined lines with a markedly sculpted head and a very obvious lower orbital chiseling, elements which all contribute to give distinction to this breed.

Important Proportions

Length of the body is the same or a little more than the height at the withers. Length of head is equal to four-tenths of the height at the withers, its width, measured at the level of the zygomatic arches, is less than half its length. Skull and muzzle are of equal length.

Behavior and Temperament

Tough and adapted to all types of hunting, reliable, endowed with an excellent ability to understand, docile and easy to train.

Head

Angular and narrow at the level of the zygomatic arches, its length corresponds to four-tenths of the height at the withers; the middle of its length is at the level of a line which unites the inner angles of both eyes; the upper longitudinal axes of the skull and muzzle are divergent, i.e., if extended, the top line of the muzzle emerges in front of the occipital protuberance, ideally at mid-length of the skull.

Skull Region

Seen in profile, the skull shape is a very open arch. Seen from the top, it forms lengthwise an elongated ellipse. The width of the skull, measured at the level of the zygomatic arches should not

The muzzle accounts for half of the head's length, with the nose protruding slightly over the lips.

An example of how form and function work together: the pendant ears and facial skin serve to gather scent and direct it to the Bracco's large nose.

exceed half of the length of the head. Cheeks are lean, the bulge of the forehead and the supraorbital ridges are perceptible, whereas the stop is not pronounced. The frontal groove is visible and ends at mid-length of the skull. The interparietal crest is short and not very prominent. The occipital protuberance is pronounced.

Facial Region
Nose—Voluminous, with large well-opened nostrils, protrudes slightly over the lips with which it forms an angle. Color brown or from pale pink to more or less deep fleshy red depending on the color of the coat. **Muzzle**—Foreface either straight or slightly arched. Its length is equal to half of the length of the head and its depth measures four-fifths of its length. Seen from the front, the lateral sides of the muzzle converge slightly, still presenting a foreface of good width. The chin not very apparent. **Lips**—Upper lips well developed, thin and floppy without being flaccid, covering the jaw; seen in profile, they overlap the lower jaw slightly, seen from the front, they form an inverted "V" below the nose; the corner of the lips must be marked without being droopy. **Teeth**—Dental arches well adapted, with the teeth square to the jaw; **scissors bite**—pincer bite is also acceptable. **Eyes**—Semi-lateral position with a soft and submissive expression neither deep set nor prominent. Eyes fairly large, eyelids oval-shaped and close-fitting (no entropion or ectropion). The iris is of a more or less dark ochre or brown color depending on the coat color. **Ears**—Well developed, in length they should, without being stretched, reach the tip of the nose. Their width is at least equal to half their length; raised only very slightly; base rather narrow, set rather backwards at level of zygomatic arches; a supple ear with a front rim well turned inwards and really close to the cheek is appreciated; the lower extremity of the ear ends in a slightly rounded tip.

Neck

Powerful, in truncated cone shape, length not less than two-thirds of the length of the head, well detached from the nape. The throat shows a soft double dewlap.

Body

Topline—The upper profile of the back is made up of two lines: one, almost straight, slopes from the withers to the 11th dorsal vertebra; the other is slightly arched, joining with the line of the rump. **Withers**—Well defined, with the points of the shoulder blades well separated. **Loin**—Wide lumbar region, muscled, short and slightly convex. **Rump**— Long (about one-third of the height at the withers), broad and well muscled; the pelvic angulation (angle formed by the pelvic girdle with a horizontal line) is 30°. Pelvis wide. **Chest**—Broad, deep and well down to level of elbows, without forming a heel, with well sprung ribs, particularly in their lower part, and sloping. **Underline**—Lower profile almost horizontal in its rib cage part, rising slightly in its abdominal part. **Tail**—Thick at the base, straight, with a slight tendency to taper, hair short. When the dog is in action and especially when questing, is carried horizontally or

The teeth should be square to the jaw with a scissors or pincer bite, although the scissors bite is preferable.

BRACCO ITALIANO

The breed standard clearly defines the correct bodily structure and proportions of the Bracco. The overall appearance is one of strength and musculature.

nearly. Should be docked at 15–25 cm from the root.

LIMBS
Forequarters—Shoulder strong, well muscled, long and sloping, very free in its movement; the upper arm sloping, fitting to the rib cage; forearm strong, straight, with strong and well marked sinews; the point of the elbows should be on a perpendicular line from the rear point of the shoulder blade to the ground; metacarpus (pasterns) well proportioned, lean, of good length and slightly sloping; feet strong, slightly oval shaped, well arched and closed toes with strong nails well curved towards the ground. Color of nails is white, yellow or brown, of a more or less dark shade depending on the color of the coat: pads elastic and lean.
Hindquarters—Thigh long, parallel, muscular, with a rear edge almost straight; strong limbs; hocks wide, metatarsals relatively short and lean. The feet, with all the characteristics of the front

Breed Standard   33

The Bracco's chest is broad and deep, reaching to the level of the elbows. The underline rises at the abdomen, and the topline is straight until it slopes at the rump.

FAULTS IN PROFILE

Generally too heavy and coarse, short neck, heavy upright shoulders, too wide in front, tail carriage too high, lacking sufficient angulation behind, improper level topline.

Generally lacking bone and substance, upright shoulders, weak pasterns, dip behind withers, exaggerated arch over loin, low tail set.

Poorly balanced, long and low on leg, upright shoulders, weak pasterns, flat feet, tail docked too short.

Generally lacking bone and substance, sloping topline, upright shoulders, ewe-necked, weak pasterns and flat feet, narrow rear, lacking sufficient angulation behind, muzzle short, weak underjaw.

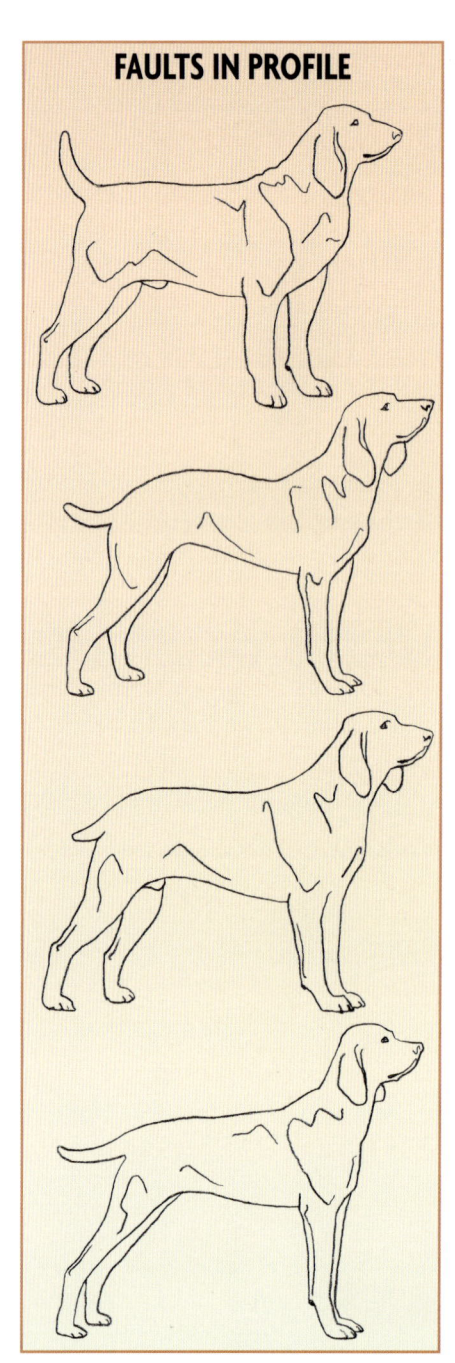

feet, have dewclaws, the absence of which is not a fault. Double dewclaw is tolerated.

Gait/Movement
Extended and fast trot, with powerful impulsion from the hindquarters; head raised, nose held high in such a way that, when hunting, the nose is higher than the topline.

Skin
Tough but elastic: fine on the head, the throat, inside the elbows and on lower part of the body. The visible mucous membranes must be a corresponding color with the coat, but never show black spots. The mucous membranes of the mouth are pink; in the roans or white and chestnut colored dogs they sometimes show brown or light chestnut spotting.

Coat
Type of hair—Short, dense and glossy, fine and shorter on the head, the ears, front part of the legs and feet. **Color of coat**—White; white with marking of varied size of an orange or more or less dark amber color, white with more or less large chestnut marking; white with pale orange (speckled); white mottled with chestnut (roan-chestnut); in this last combination, a metallic sheen is appreciated, and a warm shade of chestnut is

A trio of Bracco bitches. Females are typically a bit shorter than males, with weight in both sexes being proportionate to height.

preferred, recalling the color of a monk's tunic. A symmetrical facial mask is preferred but the absence of a mask is tolerated.

SIZE AND WEIGHT
Height at the withers between 55–67 cm. Preferred size for males: 58–67 cm; preferred size for females: 55–62 cm. Weight between 25 and 40 kg, depending on height.

FAULTS
Any departure from the foregoing constitutes a fault which when judging must be penalized according to its seriousness and its extension. **Elimination faults**—Accentuated prognathism. Size 2 cm above or below limits indicated in the standard.
Disqualifying faults—Split nose; convergence of cranial-facial axes; wall eye; upper prognathism; absence of pigmentation (albinism); black coat; white and black; tricolor; fawn, hazel, unicolor, with tan markings, mucous membranes, skin and annexes with traces of black.
N.B.: Males should have two apparently normal testicles fully descended into the scrotum.

YOUR PUPPY
BRACCO ITALIANO

PUPPY APPEARANCE
Your puppy should have a well-fed appearance but not a distended abdomen, which may indicate worms or incorrect feeding, or both. The body should be firm, with a solid feel. The skin of the abdomen should be pale pink and clean, without signs of scratching or rash.

HOW TO SELECT A PUPPY
Before reaching the decision that you will begin your search for a Bracco Italiano puppy, it is essential that you are fully clear in your mind that this is absolutely the most suitable breed for you and your family. You also need to have made a decision as to why you want a Bracco, whether as a pet, as a show dog, for field trials or some other kind of work or, more likely, a combination of some or all of these. This should be made clear to the breeder when you make your initial inquiries. If selecting for the show ring or for field work, you will need to take the breeder's advice as to which available puppy shows the most promise. If selecting a pet only, you will still need the breeder's advice to guide you to the pup whose personality best matches yours and your lifestyle.

You should have done plenty of research on the breed, and have taken advantage of every available opportunity to see and learn more about this numerically small breed. If you are truly dedicated, this may also involve visits to other countries to give yourself more exposure to Bracchi.

Choosing a breeder is an important first step in dog ownership and, with the Bracco's being so rare in most countries, this will require some searching on your part. Clubs that recognize the Bracco, as well as breed clubs like the North American Bracco Italiano Club, can be great sources of help and point you in the direction of reputable, ethical breeders. Many people in North America even look overseas for their Bracchi. Luckily, in a numerically small breed, you can trust that the majority of breeders is responsible, with the best interests of the breed in mind.

Potential owners are encouraged to attend dog shows (or trials) in which the breed is entered to see Bracchi in action, to meet the owners and handlers firsthand and to get an idea of what Bracchi look like outside a photographer's lens. Provided you approach the handlers when they are not busy with the dogs, most are more than willing to answer questions, recommend breeders and give advice about the breed they love.

Once you have contacted and met a breeder or two and made your choice about which breeder is best suited to your needs, it's time to visit the litter if the location is feasible. If the breeder is too far away for you to visit, the breeder should have photos and even videos of the litter and the parents for you to view. And be prepared to wait for a puppy! Litter sizes vary considerably;

Seeing an irresistible pile of snuggling puppies is part of the fun of visiting the litter.

YOUR SCHEDULE...

If you lead an erratic, unpredictable life, with daily or weekly changes in your work requirements, consider the problems of owning a puppy. The new puppy has to be fed regularly, socialized (loved, petted, handled, introduced to other people) and, most importantly, allowed to go outdoors for housebreaking. As the dog gets older, he can be more tolerant of deviations in his feeding and relief schedule.

three to eight pups is average, but there can be more or fewer. In such a rare breed, litters do not happen all that frequently and breeders may already have people waiting for their pups. But if you have your heart set on the Bracco, it will be worth the wait.

Remember that the dog you select should remain with you for the duration of his life, which is usually around 12 years, so making the right decision from the outset is of utmost importance. No dog should be moved from one home to another simply because his owners were thoughtless enough not to have done sufficient research and thought things through carefully before selecting the breed. It is also always important to remember that, when looking for a puppy, a good breeder will be assessing you as a prospective new owner just a carefully as you are selecting him as the breeder.

Puppies almost invariably look enchanting, but you must select one from a caring breeder who has given the puppies all the attention they deserve and has looked after them well. They should already have been well socialized, which should be apparent when you see them. Always be certain that your chosen puppy has a sound personality. He should under no circumstances show any sign of aggression, but should have an inquisitive nature and should be full of bounce. Never take pity on an unduly shy puppy, for, in doing so, you will be asking for trouble in the long run, as such a dog is likely to have problems socializing.

The puppy you select should look well fed, but not pot-bellied, as this might indicate worms. His eyes should look bright and clear, without

PEDIGREE VS. REGISTRATION CERTIFICATE

Too often new owners are confused between these two important documents. Your puppy's pedigree, essentially a family tree, is a written record of a dog's genealogy of three generations or more. The pedigree will show you the names as well as performance titles of all dogs in your pup's background. Your breeder must provide you with a registration application, with his part properly filled out. You must complete the application and send it to the registering kennel club with the proper fee.

The seller must provide you with complete records to identify the puppy. The information includes the following: breed; sex, color and markings; date of birth; litter number (when available); names and registration numbers of the parents; breeder's name; and date sold or delivered.

discharge. His nose should be moist, an indication of good health, but should never be runny. It goes without saying that there should certainly be no evidence of loose motions or parasites. The puppy you choose should also have a healthy-looking coat, an important indicator of good health internally. Always check the bite of your selected puppy to be sure that it is neither overshot nor undershot. This may not be too noticeable on a young puppy, but will become more evident as the puppy gets older. Remember that the Bracco should have a scissors bite, although a pincer bite is acceptable; overshot and undershot bites are not only undesirable, they can cause difficulty to the dog.

Before visiting the litter, you should have discussed with your family if you'd prefer a male or a female puppy, or maybe this is not important and you'd rather just see which puppy appeals to you, regardless of gender. In this breed, it is mainly a matter of personal preference, as the main difference between the two genders is in size. Because there is such a wide variation in size across the breed, it is possible to come across some bitches that are larger than their male counterparts. However, in Europe, the maximum preferred height for males is more than that of bitches, and the minimum preferred height of bitches is less than that of males.

Something else to consider when bringing home your pup is whether or not to take out

Being a puppy and watching over a litter are equally exhausting, as illustrated in this serene photo of Bracchi at rest.

> ### "YOU BETTER SHOP AROUND!"
> Finding a reputable breeder who sells healthy pups is very important, but make sure that the breeder you choose is not only someone you respect but also someone with whom you feel comfortable. Your breeder will be a resource long after you buy your puppy, and you must be able to call with reasonable questions without being made to feel like a pest! If you don't connect on a personal level, investigate some other breeders before making a final decision.
>
> If the breeder from whom you are buying a puppy asks you a lot of personal questions, do not be insulted. Such a breeder wants to be sure that you will be a fit provider for his puppy.

veterinary insurance. Vet's bills can mount up, and you must always be certain that sufficient funds are available to give your dog any veterinary attention that may be needed. To what extent your dog's health is covered will vary depending on the type of policy you select; many options are now available as veterinary insurance is growing in popularity and becoming more common.

> **TEMPERAMENT COUNTS**
> Your selection of a good puppy can be determined by your needs. A show potential or a good pet? It is your choice. Every puppy, however, should be of good temperament. Although show-quality puppies are bred and raised with emphasis on physical conformation, responsible breeders strive for equally good temperament. Do not buy from a breeder who concentrates solely on physical beauty at the expense of personality.

COMMITMENT OF OWNERSHIP

After considering all of the factors that go into selecting your puppy, you have most likely already made some very important decisions. You have chosen the Bracco Italiano, which means that you have decided which characteristics you want in a dog and what type of dog will best fit into your family and lifestyle. If you have selected a breeder, you have gone a step further—you have done your research and found a responsible, conscientious person who breeds quality Bracchi and who should be a reliable source of help as you and your puppy adjust to life together. If you have observed a litter in action, you have obtained a firsthand look at the dynamics of a puppy "pack" and, thus, you have learned about each pup's individual personality—perhaps you have even found one that particularly appeals to you.

However, even if you have not yet found the Bracco puppy of your dreams, observing pups will help you learn to recognize certain behavior and to determine what a pup's behavior indicates about his temperament. You will be able to pick out which pups are the leaders, which ones are less outgoing, which ones are confident, shy, playful, friendly, aggressive, etc.

Equally as important, you will learn to recognize what a healthy pup should look and act like. All of these things will help you in your search, and when you find the Bracco that was meant for you, you will know it!

Researching your breed, selecting a responsible breeder and observing as many pups as possible are all important steps on the way to dog ownership. It may seem like a lot of effort... and you have not even taken the pup home yet! Remember, though, you cannot be too careful when it comes to deciding on the type of dog you want and finding out about your prospective pup's background. Buying a puppy is not—or *should* not be— just another whimsical purchase. This is one instance in which you actually do get to choose your own family! You may be thinking that buying a puppy should be fun—it should not be so serious and so much work.

> **TRAINING TIP**
>
> Training your puppy takes much patience and can be frustrating at times, but you should see results from your efforts. If you have a puppy that seems untrainable, take him to a trainer or behaviorist. The dog may have a personality problem that requires the help of a professional, or perhaps you need help in learning how to train your dog.

Watching the pups interact with the breeder tells a lot about how well the pups are cared for. The pups should be eager to follow their leader and act affectionately toward her.

Keep in mind that your puppy is not a cuddly stuffed toy or decorative lawn ornament; rather, he is a living creature that will become a real member of your family. You will come to realize that, while buying a puppy is a pleasurable and exciting endeavor, it is not something to be taken lightly. Relax...the fun will start when the pup comes home!

Always keep in mind that a puppy is nothing more than a baby in a furry disguise...a baby who is virtually helpless in a human world and who trusts his owner for fulfillment of his basic

ARE YOU PREPARED?

Unfortunately, when a puppy is bought by someone who does not take into consideration the time and attention that dog ownership requires, it is the puppy who suffers when he is either abandoned or placed in a shelter by a frustrated owner. So all of the "homework" you do in preparation for your pup's arrival will benefit you both. The more informed you are, the more you will know what to expect and the better equipped you will be to handle the ups and downs of raising a puppy. Hopefully, everyone in the household is willing to do his part in raising and caring for the pup. The anticipation of owning a dog often brings a lot of promises from excited family members: "I will walk him every day," "I will feed him," "I will housebreak him," etc., but these things take time and effort, and promises can easily be forgotten once the novelty of the new pet has worn off.

needs for survival. In addition to food, water and shelter, your pup needs care, protection, guidance and love. If you are not prepared to commit to this, then you are not prepared to own a dog.

"Wait a minute," you say. "How hard could this be? All of my neighbors own dogs and they seem to be doing just fine. Why should I have to worry about all of this?" Well, you should not worry about it; in fact, you will probably find that once your Bracco pup gets used to his new home, he will fall into his place in the family quite naturally. However, it never hurts to emphasize the commitment of dog ownership. With some time and patience, it is really not too difficult to raise a curious and exuberant Bracco Italiano pup to be a well-adjusted and well-mannered adult dog—a dog that could be your most loyal friend.

PREPARING PUPPY'S PLACE IN YOUR HOME

Researching your breed and finding a breeder are only two aspects of the "homework" you will have to do before taking your Bracco puppy home. You will also have to prepare your home and family for the new addition. Much as you would prepare a nursery for a newborn baby, you will need to designate a place in your home that will be the puppy's own. How you prepare your home will depend on how much freedom the dog will be allowed. Whatever you decide, you must ensure that he has a place that he can "call his own."

When you take your new puppy into your home, you are bringing him into what will become his home as well. Obviously, you did not buy a puppy with the intentions of catering to his every whim and allowing him to "rule the roost," but in order for a puppy to grow into a stable, well-adjusted dog, he has to feel comfortable in his surroundings. Remember, he is leaving the warmth and security of his mother and littermates, as well as the familiarity of the only place he has ever known, so it is important to make his transition as easy as possible. By preparing a place in your home for the puppy, you are making him feel as welcome as possible in a strange new place. It should not take him long to get used to it, but the sudden shock of being transplanted is somewhat traumatic for a young pup. Imagine how a small child would feel in the same situation—that is how your puppy must be feeling. It is up to you to reassure him and to let him know, "Little fellow, you are going to like it here!"

TIME TO GO HOME
Breeders rarely release puppies until they are eight to ten weeks of age. This is an acceptable age for most breeds of dog, excepting Toy breeds, which are not released until around 12 weeks, given their petite sizes. If a breeder has a puppy that is 12 weeks of age or older, he is likely well socialized and house-trained. Be sure that he is otherwise healthy before deciding to take him home.

A litter of hungry puppies is a full-time job for the Bracco mom!

WHAT YOU SHOULD BUY

CRATE
To someone unfamiliar with the use of crates in dog training, it may seem like punishment to shut a dog in a crate, but this is not the case at all. More and more breeders and trainers are recommending crates as preferred tools for show puppies and pet puppies alike. Crates are not cruel—crates have many humane and highly effective uses in dog care and training. For example, crate training is a popular and very successful house-training method. In addition, a crate can keep your dog safe during travel and, perhaps most importantly, a crate provides your dog with a place of his own in your home. It serves as a "doggie bedroom" of sorts—your Bracco can curl up in his crate when he wants to

Your local pet shop should have a wide variety of crates. Choose a crate that will comfortably house the adult Bracco, keeping in mind that they can reach over 26 inches at the shoulder when full grown.

sleep or when he just needs a break. Many dogs sleep in their crates overnight. With soft bedding and his favorite toy, a crate becomes a cozy pseudo-den for your dog. Like his ancestors, he too will seek out the comfort and retreat of a den—you just happen to be providing him with something a little more luxurious than what his early ancestors enjoyed.

As far as purchasing a crate, the type that you buy is up to you. It will most likely be one of the two most popular types: wire or fiberglass. There are advantages and disadvantages to each type. For example, a wire crate is more open, allowing the air to flow through and affording the dog a view of what is going on around him, while a fiberglass crate is sturdier. Both can double as travel crates, providing protection for the dog in the car.

The size of the crate is another thing to consider. Puppies do not stay puppies forever—in fact, sometimes it seems as if they grow right before your eyes. A small crate may be fine for a very young Bracco pup, but it will not do him much good for long! Unless you have the money and the inclination to buy a new crate every time your pup has a growth spurt, it is better to get one that will accommodate your dog both as a pup and at full size. A large or giant-sized crate will be necessary to comfortably house your adult Bracco Italiano.

BEDDING

A soft crate pad and perhaps a blanket in the dog's crate will help the dog feel more at home. First, this bedding will take the place of the leaves, twigs, etc. that the pup would use in the wild to make a den; the pup can make his own "burrow" in the crate. Although your pup is far removed from his den-making ancestors, the denning instinct is still a part of his genetic makeup. Second, until you take your pup home, he has been sleeping amid the warmth of his mother and littermates, and while a blanket is not the same as a warm, breathing body, it still provides heat and something with which to snuggle. You will want to wash your pup's bedding frequently in case he has a potty accident in his crate, and replace or remove any blanket or padding that becomes ragged and starts to fall apart.

Toys

Toys are a must for dogs of all ages, especially for curious playful pups. Puppies are the "children" of the dog world, and what child does not love toys? Chew toys provide enjoyment for both dog and owner—your dog will enjoy playing with his favorite toys, while you will enjoy the fact that they distract him from chewing on your expensive shoes and leather sofa. Puppies love to chew; in fact, chewing is a physical need for pups as they are teething, and everything looks appetizing! The full range of your possessions—from dish rag to Oriental carpet—are fair game in the eyes of a teething pup. Puppies are not all that discerning when it comes to finding something literally to "sink their teeth into"—everything tastes great!

The Bracco Italiano is not known as a particularly aggressive chewer, but he will enjoy toys. Any toys you offer to your Bracco should be utterly safe, with no removable parts. Highly durable toys and chews are

TOYS, TOYS, TOYS!
With a big variety of dog toys available, and so many that look like they would be a lot of fun for a dog, be careful in your selection. It is amazing what a set of puppy teeth can do to an innocent-looking toy, so, obviously, safety is a major consideration. Be sure to choose the most durable products that you can find. Hard nylon bones and toys are a safe bet, and many of them are offered in different scents and flavors that will be sure to capture your dog's attention. It is always fun to play a game of fetch with your dog, and there are balls and flying discs that are specially made to withstand dog teeth.

Your local pet shop will have a variety of leads from which you can choose a suitable sturdy lead for your Bracco.

essential, and balls should never be so small that they might be swallowed accidentally.

Breeders advise owners to resist stuffed toys, because they can become de-stuffed in no time. The overly excited pup may ingest the stuffing, which is neither nutritious nor digestible. Similarly, squeaky toys are quite popular, but must be avoided for the Bracco. Perhaps a squeaky toy can be used as an aid in training, but not for free play. If a pup "disembowels" one of these, the small plastic squeaker inside can be dangerous if swallowed. Monitor the condition of all your pup's toys carefully and get rid of any that have been chewed to the point of becoming potentially dangerous.

Be careful of natural bones, which have a tendency to splinter into sharp, dangerous pieces. Also be careful of rawhide, which can turn into pieces that are easy to swallow and become a mushy mess on your carpet.

Lead

A nylon lead is probably the best option, as it is the most resistant to puppy teeth should your pup take a liking to chewing on his lead. Of course, this is a habit that should be nipped in the bud, but, if your pup likes to chew on his lead, he has a very slim chance of being able to chew through the strong nylon. Nylon leads are also lightweight, which is good for a young Bracco who is just getting used to the idea of walking on a lead. For everyday walking and safety purposes, the nylon lead is a good choice for the pup.

As your pup grows up and into a large, strong dog, you will need a stronger lead as well. A thicker nylon or leather lead will suit an adult Bracco.

Collar

Your pup should get used to wearing a collar all the time since you will want to attach his ID tags to it; plus, you have to attach the lead to something! A lightweight nylon collar is a good choice. Make certain that the collar fits snugly enough so that the pup cannot wriggle out

CHOOSE AN APPROPRIATE COLLAR

The **BUCKLE COLLAR** is the standard collar used for everyday purposes. Be sure that you adjust the buckle on growing puppies. Check it every day. It can become too tight overnight! These collars can be made of leather or nylon. Attach your dog's identification tags to this collar.

The **CHOKE COLLAR** is designed for training. It is constructed of highly polished steel so that it slides easily through the stainless steel loop. The idea is that the dog controls the pressure around his neck and he will stop pulling if the collar becomes uncomfortable. It is *not* a suitable device for the Bracco.

The **HALTER** is for a trained dog that has to be restrained to prevent running away, chasing a cat and the like. Considered the most humane of all collars, it is frequently used on smaller dogs on which collars are not comfortable.

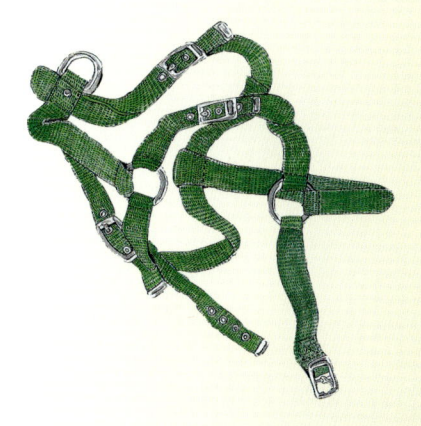

Choose durable, easily cleaned bowls of appropriate size. Also important are stands on which to elevate your dog's bowls; these should be considered mandatory to serve as a bloat preventative for the deep-chested Bracco.

of it, but is loose enough so that it will not be uncomfortably tight around the pup's neck. You should be able to fit a finger between the pup's neck and the collar. It may take some time for your pup to get used to wearing the collar, but soon he will not even notice that it is there. Choke collars are made for training, but are neither necessary nor recommended for the Bracco, as they do not respond well to negative or harsh training methods. Plus, the dewlap around the breed's neck prevents the use of this type of collar.

FOOD AND WATER BOWLS

Your pup will need two bowls, one for food and one for water. You may want two sets of bowls, one for indoors and one for outdoors, depending on where the dog will be fed and where he will be spending time. Stainless steel or sturdy plastic bowls are popular choices. Plastic bowls are more chewable, but dogs tend not to chew on the steel variety, which can be sterilized. It is important to buy sturdy bowls since anything is in danger of being chewed by puppy teeth and you do not want your dog to be constantly chewing apart his bowl (for his safety and for your purse!).

An important bloat preventative is to serve your dog's meals and water in elevated bowls. Elevating the food and water to the dog's level reduces the risk of his swallowing air while eating and drinking, thus reducing the risk of his developing bloat. Bowl stands can be purchased wherever you buy pet supplies. Consider this a necessary investment in your Bracco Italiano's good health and long life!

CLEANING SUPPLIES
Until a pup is house-trained, you will be doing a lot of cleaning. Potty accidents will occur, which is acceptable in the beginning stages of toilet training because the puppy does not know any better. All you can do is be prepared to clean up any accidents as soon as they happen. Old rags, paper towels, newspapers and a safe disinfectant are good to have on hand.

BEYOND THE BASICS
The items previously discussed are the bare necessities. You will find out what else you need as you go along—grooming supplies, flea/tick protection, baby gates to partition a room, etc. These things will vary depending on your situation, but it is important that you have everything you need to feed and make your Bracco Italiano comfortable in his first few days at home.

It is your responsibility to clean up after your dog has relieved himself. Pet shops have various aids to assist in the cleanup job.

PUPPY-PROOFING YOUR HOME
Aside from making sure that your Bracco will be comfortable in your home, you also have to make sure that your home is safe for your Bracco. This means taking precautions that your pup will not get into anything he should not get into and that there is nothing within his reach that may harm him should he sniff it, chew it, inspect it, etc. This probably seems obvious since, while you are primarily concerned with your pup's safety, at the same time you do not want your belongings to be ruined. Breakables should be

NATURAL TOXINS

Examine your grass and landscaping before bringing your puppy home. Many varieties of plants have leaves, stems or flowers that are toxic if ingested, and you can depend on a curious puppy to investigate them. Ask your vet for information on poisonous plants or research them at your library.

If you see your dog carrying a piece of vegetation in his mouth, approach him in a quiet, disinterested manner, avoid eye contact, pet him and gradually remove the plant from his mouth. Alternatively, offer him a treat and maybe he'll drop the plant on his own accord. Be sure no toxic plants are growing in your own yard or kept in your home.

placed out of reach if your dog is to have full run of the house. If he is to be limited to certain places within the house, keep any potentially dangerous items in the "off-limits" areas.

An electrical cord can pose a danger should the puppy decide to taste it—and who is going to convince a pup that it would not make a great chew toy? All cords and wires should be fastened tightly against the wall, out of the pup's sight and away from his reach. If your dog is going to spend time in a crate, make sure that there is nothing near his crate that he can reach if he sticks his curious little nose or paws through the openings. Just as you would with a child, keep all household cleaners and chemicals where the pup cannot reach them.

It is also important to make sure that the outside of your home is safe. Of course, your puppy should never be unsupervised, but a pup let loose in the yard will want to run and explore, and he should be granted that freedom. Do not let a fence give you a false sense of security; you would be surprised at how crafty (and persistent) a dog can be in working out how to dig under and squeeze his way through small holes, or to jump or climb over a fence. Individual Bracchi vary in their desire to "escape," but they are certainly capable of digging, climbing or jumping their way out of a yard. A sturdy fence, at least 6 feet high, would be sensible, and make sure that the fence is well embedded into the ground.

Be sure to secure any gaps in the fence. Check the fence periodically to ensure that it is in good shape and make repairs as needed. A very determined pup may return to the same spot to "work on it" until he is able to get through.

FIRST TRIP TO THE VET
You have selected your puppy, and your home and family are ready. Now all you have to do is collect your Bracco Italiano from the breeder and the fun begins, right? Well…not so fast. Something else you need to plan is your pup's first trip to the vet. Perhaps the breeder can recommend someone in the area who has had some experience with the breed or similar sporting breeds, or maybe you know some other dog owners who can suggest a good vet. Either way, you should have an appointment arranged for your pup before you pick him up.

The pup's first visit will consist of an overall examination to make sure that the pup does not have any problems that are not apparent to you. The vet will also set up a schedule for the pup's vaccinations; the breeder will inform you of which ones the pup has already received and the vet can continue from there.

INTRODUCTION TO THE FAMILY
Everyone in the house will be excited about the puppy's coming home and will want to pet him and play with him, but it is best to make the intro-

This young Bracco seems to have bitten off more than he can chew!

> **CHEMICAL TOXINS**
> Scour your garage for potential puppy dangers. Remove weed killers, pesticides and antifreeze materials. Antifreeze is highly toxic and just a few drops can kill a puppy or an adult dog. The sweet taste attracts the animal, who will quickly consume it from the floor or pavement.

ductions low-key so as not to overwhelm the puppy. He is apprehensive already. It is the first time he has been separated from his mother and the breeder, and the ride to your home is likely to be the first time he has been in a car. The last thing you want to do is smother him, as this will only frighten him further. This is not to say that human contact is not extremely necessary at this stage, because this is the time when a connection between the pup and his human family is formed. Gentle petting and soothing words should help console him, as well as just putting him down and letting him explore on his own (under your watchful eye, of course).

PET INSURANCE
Just like you can insure your car, your house and your own health, you likewise can insure your dog's health. Investigate a pet insurance policy by talking to your vet. Depending on the age of your dog, the breed and the kind of coverage you desire, your policy can be very affordable. Most policies cover accidental injuries, poisoning, and thousands of medical problems and illnesses, including cancers. Some carriers also offer routine care and immunization coverage.

The pup may approach the family members or may busy himself with exploring for a while. Gradually, each person should spend some time with the pup, one at a time, crouching down to get as close to the pup's level as possible, while letting him sniff each person's hands and petting him gently. He definitely needs human attention and he needs to be touched—this is how to form an immediate bond. Just remember that the pup is experiencing many things for the first time, at the same time. There are new people, new noises, new smells and new things to investigate, so be gentle, be affectionate and be as comforting as you can be.

PUP'S FIRST NIGHT HOME
You have traveled home with your new charge safely in his crate or on a friend's lap. He's been to the vet for a thorough check-up; he's been weighed, his papers have been examined and perhaps he's even been vaccinated and wormed as well. He's met the whole family, including the excited children and the less-than-happy cat. He's explored his area, his new bed, the yard and anywhere else he's been permitted. He's eaten his first meal at home and relieved himself in the proper place. He's heard lots of new sounds, smelled new friends and seen more of the outside

world than ever before…and that was just the first day! He's worn out and is ready for bed…or so you think!

It's puppy's first night home and you are ready to say "Good night." Keep in mind that this is his first night ever to be sleeping alone. His dam and littermates are no longer at paw's length and he's a bit scared, cold and lonely. Be reassuring to your new family member, but this is not the time to spoil him and give in to his inevitable whining.

Puppies whine. They whine to let others know where they are and hopefully to get company out of it. Place your pup in his new bed or crate in his designated area and close the crate door. Mercifully, he may fall asleep without a peep. When the inevitable occurs, however, ignore the whining—he is fine. Be strong and keep his interest in mind. Do not allow yourself to feel guilty and visit the pup. He will fall asleep eventually.

Many breeders recommend placing a piece of bedding from the pup's former home in his new bed so that he recognizes and is comforted by the scent of his littermates. Others still advise placing a hot water bottle in the bed for warmth. The latter may be a good idea provided the pup doesn't attempt to suckle—he'll get good and wet, and may not fall asleep so fast.

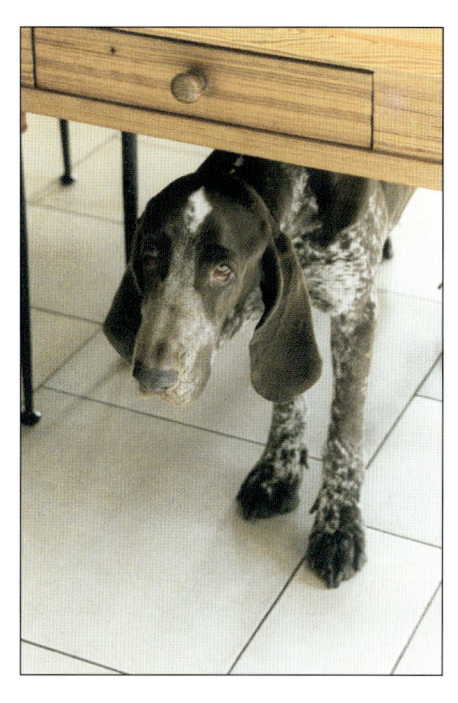

Once your Bracco is accustomed to your home, you may be surprised at where he will choose his favorite spots.

Puppy's first night can be somewhat stressful for both the pup and his new family. Remember that you are setting the tone of nighttime at your house. Unless you want to play with your pup every night at 10 p.m., midnight and 2 a.m., don't initiate the habit. Your family will thank you, and eventually so will your pup!

PREVENTING PUPPY PROBLEMS

SOCIALIZATION
Now that you have done all of the preparatory work and have helped your pup get accustomed

to his new home and family, it is about time for you to have some fun! Socializing your Bracco pup gives you the opportunity to show off your new friend—likely no one in your neighborhood has ever met this enchanting rare breed—and your pup gets to reap the benefits of being an adorable creature that people will want to pet and, in general, think is absolutely precious!

Besides getting to know his new family, your puppy should be exposed to other people, animals and situations. This will help him become well adjusted as he grows up and less prone to being timid or fearful of the new things he will encounter. Of course, he must not come into close contact with dogs you don't know well until his course of injections is fully complete.

Your pup's socialization began with the breeder, but now

The Bracco's athleticism is a big factor in providing a safe environment for your pet. It takes a little extra effort (and height!) to confine an agile Bracco!

MISCHIEF MAKER
Although in maturity, the Bracco Italiano is a very sensible sort of fellow, as a puppy he can be just as naughty as any other breed! Like others, the young Bracco can be destructive, too. It is never wise to leave a Bracco with temptation for too long a period, or you may not be happy with the outcome!

it is your responsibility to continue it. The socialization he receives until the age of 12 weeks is the most critical, as this is the time when he forms his impressions of the outside world. Be especially careful during the eight-to-ten-week-old period, also known as the fear period. The interaction he receives during this time should be gentle and reassuring. Lack of socialization, and/or negative experiences during the socialization period, can manifest itself in fear and aggression as the dog grows up. Your puppy needs lots of positive interaction, which of course includes human contact, affection, handling and exposure to other animals.

Once your pup has received his necessary vaccinations, feel free to take him out and about (on his lead, of course). Walk him around the neighborhood, take him on your daily errands, let people pet him, let him meet other dogs and pets, etc. Puppies do not have to try to make friends; there will be no shortage of people who will want to introduce themselves. Just make sure that you carefully supervise each meeting. If the neighborhood children want to say hello, for example, that is great—children and pups most often make great companions. However, sometimes an excited child can unintentionally handle a pup too roughly, or an overzealous pup can playfully nip a little too hard. You want to make socialization experiences positive ones. What a pup learns during this very formative stage will affect his attitude toward future encounters. You want your dog to be comfortable around everyone. A pup that has a bad experience with a child may grow up to be a dog that is shy around or aggressive toward children.

Consistency in Training

Dogs, being pack animals, naturally need a leader, or else they try to establish dominance in their packs. When you welcome a dog into your family, the choice of who becomes the leader and who becomes the "pack" is entirely up to you! Your pup's intuitive quest for dominance, coupled with the fact that it is nearly impossible to look at an adorable Bracco pup with his "puppy-dog" eyes

MANNERS MATTER
During the socialization process, a puppy should meet people, experience different environments and definitely be exposed to other canines. Through playing and interacting with other dogs, your puppy will learn lessons, ranging from controlling the pressure of his jaws by biting his littermates to the inner-workings of the canine pack that he will apply to his human relationships for the rest of his life. That is why removing a puppy from the litter too early (before eight weeks) can be detrimental to the pup's development.

and not cave in, give the pup almost an unfair advantage in getting the upper hand!

A pup will definitely test the waters to see what he can and cannot do. Do not give in to those pleading eyes—stand your ground when it comes to disciplining the pup and make sure that all family members do the same. It will only confuse the pup if Mother tells him to get off the sofa when he is used to sitting up there with Father to watch the nightly news. Avoid discrepancies by having all members of the household decide on the rules before the pup even comes home...and be consistent in enforcing them! Early training shapes the dog's personality, so you cannot be unclear in what you expect.

COMMON PUPPY PROBLEMS
The best way to prevent puppy problems is to be proactive in stopping an undesirable behavior as soon as it starts. The old saying "You can't teach an old dog new tricks" does not necessarily hold true, but it *is* true that it is much easier to discourage bad behavior in a young developing pup than to wait until the pup's bad behavior becomes the adult dog's bad habit. There are some problems that are especially prevalent in puppies as they develop.

NIPPING
As puppies start to teethe, they feel the need to sink their teeth into anything available...unfortunately, that usually includes your fingers, arms, hair and toes. You may find this behavior cute for the first five seconds...until you feel just how sharp those puppy teeth are. Nipping is

The Bracco enjoys the company of other dogs, a trait he inherited from his gregarious hound forefathers.

THE COCOA WARS
Chocolate contains the chemical thebromine, which is poisonous to dogs, although "chocolates" especially made for dogs are safe (as they don't actually contain chocolate) but not recommended. Any item that encourages your dog to enjoy the taste of cocoa should be discouraged. You should also exercise caution when using mulch in your garden. This frequently contains cocoa hulls, and dogs have been known to die from eating mulch.

Puppy

Is it time for a walk or time for a chew? With puppies, almost any time is time for a chew!

something you want to discourage immediately and consistently with a firm "No!" (or whatever number of firm "Nos" it takes for him to understand that you mean business). Then, replace your finger with an appropriate chew toy. While this behavior is merely annoying when the dog is young, it can become dangerous as your Bracco's adult teeth grow in and his jaws develop, and he continues to think it is okay to gnaw on human appendages. Your Bracco does not mean any harm with a friendly nip, but he also does not know his own strength.

Crying/Whining

Your pup will often cry, whine, whimper, howl or make some type of commotion when he is left alone. This is basically his way of calling out for attention to make sure that you know he is there and that you have not forgotten about him. Your puppy feels insecure when he is left alone, when you are out of the house and he is in his crate or when you are in another part of

> **PUP MEETS WORLD**
>
> Thorough socialization includes not only meeting new people but also being introduced to new experiences such as riding in the car, having his coat brushed, hearing the television, walking in a crowd—the list is endless. The more your pup experiences, and the more positive the experiences are, the less of a shock and the less frightening it will be for your pup to encounter new things.

CHEWING TIPS

Chewing goes hand in hand with nipping in the sense that a teething puppy is always looking for a way to soothe his aching gums. In this case, instead of chewing on you, he may have taken a liking to your favorite shoe or something else that he should not be chewing. Again, realize that this is a normal canine behavior that does not need to be discouraged, only redirected. Your pup just needs to be taught what is acceptable to chew on and what is off-limits. Consistently tell him "No!" when you catch him chewing on something forbidden and give him a chew toy.

Conversely, praise him when you catch him chewing on something appropriate. In this way, you are discouraging the inappropriate behavior and reinforcing the desired behavior. The puppy's chewing should stop after his adult teeth have come in, but an adult dog continues to chew for various reasons—perhaps because he is bored, needs to relieve tension or just likes to chew. That is why it is important to redirect his chewing when he is still young.

---

the house and he cannot see you. The noise he is making is an expression of the anxiety he feels at being alone, so he needs to be taught that being alone is okay. You are not actually training the dog to stop making noise; rather, you are training him to feel comfortable when he is alone and thus removing the need for him to make the noise.

This is where the crate with cozy bedding and a toy comes in handy. You want to know that your pup is safe when you are not there to supervise, and you know that he will be safe in his crate rather than roaming freely about the house. In order for the pup to stay in his crate without making a fuss, he first needs to be comfortable in his crate. On that note, it is extremely important that the crate is never used as a form of punishment; this will cause the pup to view the crate as a negative place, rather than as a place of his own for safety and retreat.

Accustom the pup to the crate in short, gradually increasing time intervals in which you put him in the crate, maybe with a treat, and stay in the room with him. If he cries or makes a fuss, do not go to him, but stay in his sight. Gradually he will realize that staying in his crate is just fine without your help, and it will not be so traumatic for him when you are not around. You may want to leave the radio on softly when you leave the house; the sound of human voices may be comforting to him.

EVERYDAY CARE OF YOUR BRACCO ITALIANO

FEEDING YOUR BRACCO
Bracchi are usually good eaters, but, especially as puppies, they require a sensible high-quality diet to aid the correct formation of bones and joints. In adulthood, protein content will vary according to whether or not the dog lives an especially active lifestyle. When purchasing a puppy, a carefully selected breeder should be able to give good advice in this regard.

An owner should never be tempted to allow a dog to put on too much weight, for an overweight dog is more prone to health problems than one that is of correct weight. Feeding any dog tidbits between meals will run the risk of having an unhealthy, over-weight dog in maturity. Carrots are an excellent treat for a dog, for they will not put on weight and, in addition, will help to keep teeth clean.

Many owners like to feed two meals each day, others just one. However frequently you decide to feed your dog, remember that no dog should ever be fed within at least an hour (before or after) of strenuous exercise; indeed, some owners like to allow a two-hour lapse between feeding and exercise.

There are now numerous high-quality canine meals available, and one of them is sure to suit your own Bracco. Once again, you

TEST FOR PROPER DIET
A good test for proper diet is the color, odor and firmness of your dog's stool. A healthy dog usually produces three semi-hard stools per day. The stools should have no unpleasant odor. They should be the same color from excretion to excretion.

FOOD PREFERENCE

Selecting the best dog food is difficult. There is no majority consensus among veterinary scientists as to the value of nutrient analysis (protein, fat, fiber, moisture, ash, cholesterol, minerals, etc.). All agree that feeding trials are what matter most, but you also have to consider the individual dog. The dog's weight, age and activity level, and what pleases his taste, all must be considered. It is best to take the advice of your veterinarian. Every dog's dietary requirements vary, even during the lifetime of a particular dog.

If your dog is fed a good dry food, he does not require supplements of meat or vegetables. Dogs do appreciate a little variety in their diets, so you may choose to stay with the same brand but vary the flavor. Alternatively, you may wish to add a little flavored stock to give a difference to the taste.

should be able to obtain sound advice from your dog's breeder as to which food is considered most suitable. The breeder will have knowledge of with which foods he has had success in his own dogs. When you brought your puppy home, the breeder should have provided you with a diet sheet, giving details of exactly how your puppy was fed up to that point. Of course, you will be at liberty to change that food, together with the frequency and timing of meals, as the youngster reaches adulthood, but this should be done gradually.

Some owners still prefer to feed fresh food, instead of one of the more convenient complete diets. There are so many complete commercially prepared foods now available, some scientifically balanced, that a lot will depend on personal preference. Although you have to be very careful not to unbalance an otherwise balanced diet, if you are unfortunate enough to have the rare finicky eater, sometimes a little added fresh meat, or even just gravy or stock, will gain your Bracco's interest and stimulate his appetite.

Dog foods are produced in three basic types: dry, semi-moist and canned. Dry foods are useful for the cost-conscious, for overall they tend to be less expensive than semi-moist or canned foods. Dry foods also contain the least fat

Everyday Care

and the most preservatives. In general, canned foods are made up of 60–70% water, while semi-moist ones often contain so much sugar that they are perhaps the least preferred by owners, even though their dogs seem to like them.

When selecting your dog's diet, three stages of development must be considered: the puppy stage, the adult stage and the senior stage.

PUPPY STAGE

Puppies instinctively want to suck milk from their mother's teats; a normal puppy will exhibit this behavior just a few moments following birth. If puppies do not attempt to suckle within the first half-hour or so, the breeder should encourage them to do so by placing them on the nipples, having selected ones with plenty of milk. This early milk supply is important in providing the essential colostrum, which protects the puppies during the first eight to ten weeks of their lives. Although a mother's milk is much better than any commercially prepared milk formula, despite there being some excellent ones available, if the puppies do not feed, the breeder will have to feed them by hand. For those with less experience, advice from a vet is important so that not only the right quantity of milk is fed but also

There is nothing better for puppies in their first weeks of life than to nurse from their mother.

> **GRAIN-BASED DIETS**
> Some less expensive dog foods are based on grains and other plant proteins. While these products may appear to be attractively priced, many breeders prefer a diet based on animal proteins and believe that they are more conducive to your dog's health. Many grain-based diets rely on soy protein, which may cause flatulence (passing gas).
>
> There are many cases, however, when your dog might require a special diet. These special requirements should only be recommended by your veterinarian.

that of correct quality, fed at suitably frequent intervals, usually every two hours during the first few days of life.

Puppies should be allowed to nurse from their mother for about the first six weeks, although, starting around the third or fourth week, the breeder will begin to introduce small portions of suitable solid food. Most breeders like to introduce alternate milk and meat meals initially, building up to weaning time.

By the time the puppies are seven or a maximum of eight weeks old, they should be fully weaned and fed solely on a proprietary puppy food. Selection of the most suitable, good-quality diet at this time is essential, for a puppy's fastest growth rate is during the first year of life. Some brands also have a slight variation for "juniors." Consult your vet or breeder for advice in this regard.

The frequency of meals will be reduced over time, and the time at which you will switch to an adult food will vary according to the make of food used and the individual dog's bodily development. Bracchi are usually switched to an adult-maintenance food by about 10 to 12 months of age, but again, this does vary. Puppy and junior diets should be well balanced for the needs of your dog so that, except in certain circumstances, additional vitamins, minerals and proteins will not be required.

Adult Diets

A dog is considered an adult when he has stopped growing; in the Bracco, maturity will usually be reached by three years of age. However, the Bracco will begin on an adult diet at around 10 to 12 months of age, long before he's reached full maturity. Again you should rely upon your breeder or vet to recommend an acceptable maintenance diet. Major dog-food manufacturers specialize in this type of food, and it is merely necessary for you to select the one best suited to your dog's needs. Active dogs will have different requirements than sedate dogs.

Senior Diets

As dogs get older, their metabolism changes. The older dog usually exercises less, moves more slowly and sleeps more. This change in lifestyle and physiological performance requires a change in diet. Since these changes take place slowly, they might not be recognizable. What is easily recognizable is weight gain. By continuing to feed your dog an adult-maintenance diet when he is slowing down metabolically, your dog will gain weight. Obesity in an older dog compounds the health problems that already accompany old age.

As your dog gets older, few of his organs function up to par. The kidneys slow down and the intestines become less efficient. These age-related factors are best handled with a change in diet and a change in feeding schedule to give smaller portions that are more easily digested. There is no single best diet for every older dog. While many dogs do well on light or senior diets, other dogs do better on puppy diets or special premium diets such as lamb and rice. Some Bracchi are switched to a senior diet at around seven or eight years old, but others never make the switch. Be extra sensitive to your senior Bracco Italiano's diet, as this will surely help control other problems that may arise with your old friend.

FEEDING TIPS
- Dog food must be served at room temperature, neither too hot nor too cold. Fresh water, changed often and served in a clean bowl, is mandatory.
- Never feed your dog from the table while you are eating, and never feed your dog leftovers from your own meal. They usually contain too much fat and too much seasoning.
- Dogs must chew their food. Hard pellets are excellent; soups and stews are to be avoided.
- Don't add leftovers or any extras to commercial dog food. The normal food is usually balanced, and adding something extra destroys the balance.
- Except for age-related changes, dogs do not require dietary variations. They can be fed the same diet, day after day, without their becoming bored or ill.

A Worthy Investment

Veterinary studies have proven that a balanced high-quality diet pays off in your dog's coat quality, behavior and activity level. Invest in premium brands for the maximum payoff with your dog.

Everyday Care

WATER

Just as your dog needs proper nutrition from his food, water is an essential "nutrient" as well. Water keeps the dog's body properly hydrated and promotes normal function of the body's systems. During house-training, it is necessary to keep an eye on how much water your Bracco is drinking, but, once he is reliably trained, he should have access to clean fresh water at all times, especially if you feed dry food only, although it is wise to limit the dog's water intake at mealtimes as a bloat preventative. Make certain that the dog's water bowl is clean and on an elevated stand, and change the water often.

EXERCISE

The Bracco Italiano is an active breed and, thus, thoroughly enjoys exercise; indeed, this is necessary for both the Bracco's health and happiness. How a Bracco is best exercised depends very much on the area in which you live, but an on-lead walk with an opportunity for a good free run in a secure area should be a daily routine.

Free runs should, of course, only be allowed in places that are completely safe. All possible escape routes should be thoroughly checked out before letting a dog off-lead. After exercise, your Bracco should be allowed to settle

DRINK, DRANK, DRUNK—MAKE IT A DOUBLE

In both humans and dogs, as well as other living organisms, water forms the major part of nearly every body tissue. Naturally, we take water for granted, but without it, life as we know it would cease.

For dogs, water is needed to keep their bodies functioning biochemically. Additionally, water is needed to replace the water lost while panting. Unlike humans, who are able to sweat to dissipate heat, dogs must pant to cool down, thereby losing the vital water that their bodies need to regulate their body temperatures. Humans lose electrolyte-containing products and other body-fluid components through sweating; dogs do not lose anything except water.

Water is essential always, but especially so when the weather is hot or humid or when your dog is exercising or working vigorously.

down quietly for a rest, and please remember that, following exercise, at least one full hour should elapse before feeding.

Puppies, although full of bounce, should have only limited exercise during the crucial period of bone growth. Young dogs should be exercised with care, and it is unwise for youngsters to have full freedom of exercise until they are about one year old.

Bear in mind that an overweight dog should never be suddenly over-exercised; instead, he should be encouraged to increase exercise slowly. Also remember that exercise is not only essential to keep the dog's body fit, it is just as essential to his mental well-being. A bored dog will find something to do, which often manifests itself in some type of destructive behavior. In this sense, exercise is essential for the owner's mental well-being as well!

Playtime or feeding time? The puppies enjoy some fun time splashing about in the "big dog's" bowls.

THE CANINE GOURMET
Your dog does not prefer a fresh bone. Indeed, he wants it properly aged and, if given such a treat indoors, he is more likely to try to bury it in the carpet than he is to settle in for a good chew! If you have a yard, give him such delicacies outside and guide him to a place suitable for his "bone yard." He will carefully place the treasure in its earthy vault and seemingly forget about it. Trust me, his seeming distaste or lack of thanks for your thoughtfulness is not that at all. He will return in a few days to inspect the bone, perhaps to re-bury it, and when it is just right, he will relish it as much as you do that cooked-to-perfection steak. If he is in a concrete or bricked kennel run, he will be especially frustrated at the hopelessness of the situation. He will vacillate between ignoring it completely, giving it a few licks to speed the curing process with saliva, and trying to hide it behind the water bowl! When the bone has aged a bit, he will set to work on it.

GROOMING
Although a short-coated breed, to keep the Bracco's coat in good, healthy, clean condition, some grooming is essential. Plus, grooming sessions are a good way to spend time with your dog, increasing your mutual bond. Every owner will have his own preference as to what equipment

Everyday Care

suits him best, and this may be a combination of grooming gloves, chamois leathers, pure bristle brushes and rubber brushes. It is wise to get into the routine of grooming regularly, ideally short sessions on a daily basis. There will be times at which the coat will shed, at which time regular and thorough grooming is an absolute must. Special attention should be paid to any areas in which skin is plentiful.

A Bracco that has become wet when exercising in the rain should always be wiped down thoroughly with a towel, so as not to remain damp. Special attention should be paid to the underside, where mud and water can sometimes go unnoticed until it is too late and the mud has dried into the coat. In any event, never leave a dog damp in cold weather or in a draft. Provided the coat is well cared for, Bracchi only need baths occasionally,

In the event that you do need to bathe your Bracco, you should brush him thoroughly before wetting his coat. This will get rid of any dead hair in the coat, which is harder to remove when the coat is wet. Make certain that your dog has a good non-slip surface on which to stand. Begin by wetting the dog's coat, checking the water temperature to make sure that it is neither too hot nor

Your Bracco will find a way to entertain himself, so provide him with safe toys and keep an eye on his activities.

"DOES THIS COLLAR MAKE ME LOOK FAT?"

While humans may obsess about how they look and how trim their bodies are, many people believe that extra weight on their dogs is a good thing. The truth is, pets should not be over- or under-weight, as both can lead to or signal sickness. In order to tell how fit your pet is, run your hands over his ribs. Are his ribs buried under a layer of fat or are they sticking out considerably? If your pet is within his normal weight range, you should be able to feel the ribs easily, but they should not protrude abnormally. If you stand above him, the outline of his body should resemble an hourglass. Some breeds do tend to be leaner while some are a bit stockier, but making sure your dog is the right weight for his breed will certainly contribute to his good health.

BRACCO ITALIANO

Your pet shop should have all of the necessary grooming tools for maintaining your Bracco's short coat in top condition.

too cold for the dog. A shower or hose attachment is necessary for thoroughly wetting and rinsing the coat.

Next, apply shampoo to the dog's coat and work it into a good lather. Wash the head last, as you do not want shampoo to drip into the dog's eyes while you are washing the rest of his body. You should use only a shampoo that is made for dogs; never use a product made for human hair. Work the shampoo all the way down to the skin. You can use this opportunity to check the skin for any bumps, bites or other abnormalities. Do not neglect any area of the body—get all of the hard-to-reach places.

Once the dog has been thoroughly shampooed, he requires an equally thorough rinsing. Shampoo left in the coat can be irritating to the dog's skin. Protect his eyes from the shampoo by shielding them with your hand and directing the flow of water in the opposite direction. You also should avoid getting water in the ear canal. Be prepared for your dog to shake out his coat—you might want to stand back, but make sure you have a hold on the dog to keep him from running through the house and a heavy towel close at hand.

PHOTO COURTESY OF MIKKI PET PRODUCTS.

EAR CARE AND CLEANING

Because of the shape and hang of the Bracco's ears, you will always

Everyday Care 69

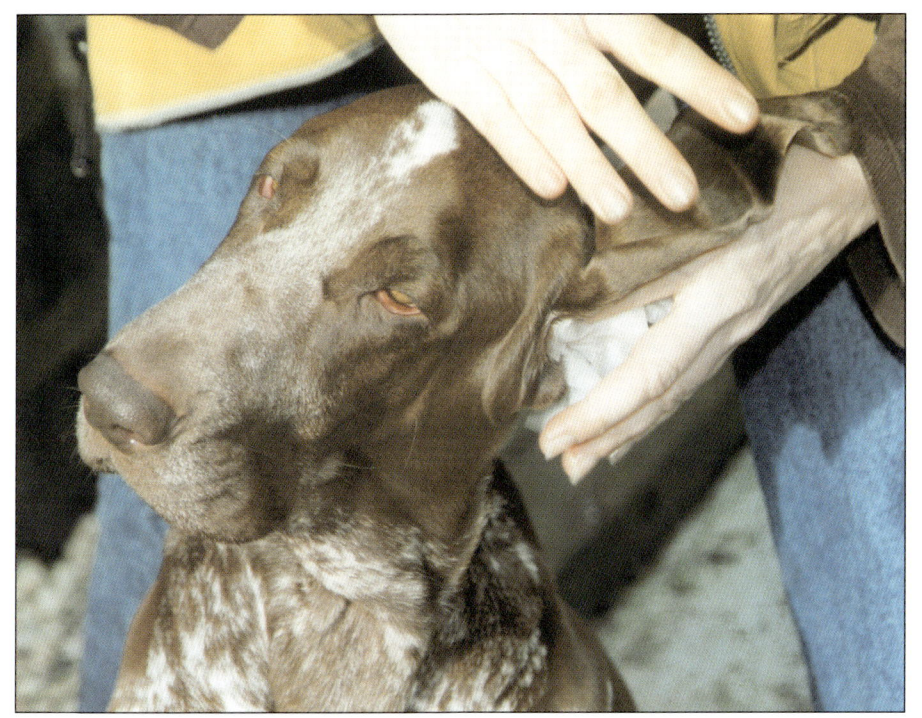

Your Bracco's long ears must be cleaned regularly. Use a soft wipe with an ear-cleaning liquid or powder made for dogs, never probing into the ear canal. Report any abnormalities to your vet.

need to pay careful attention to them. Dogs with long, hanging ears are more likely to suffer from ear problems than others. Sometimes such problems can be related to skin allergy, while other times caused by dirt or wax build-up, or ear mites. Ears should be kept clean using a special ear-cleaning liquid or powder and a cotton ball or soft wipe. Take care not to delve into the ear canal, as this might cause injury.

Always check for any sign of an unusual odor, as this most probably indicates infection or mite infestation. Likewise, a dark-brown waxy substance in the ear indicates ear mites or a similar condition, especially when combined with an odor. Such a condition can be very painful for a dog, especially if not dealt with early. The dog will scratch at his ear, indicating irritation, and in bad cases will hold his head sideways, inclining toward the affected ear.

Regular inspection of the ear will help an owner to detect any early signs of ear infection, and ears should be cleaned regularly. Unless an ear problem can be rectified immediately, veterinary attention should be sought before it worsens.

A grooming mitt or hound glove will be sufficient for grooming the Bracco's close coat, and dogs often enjoy the feel of being groomed with one of these tools.

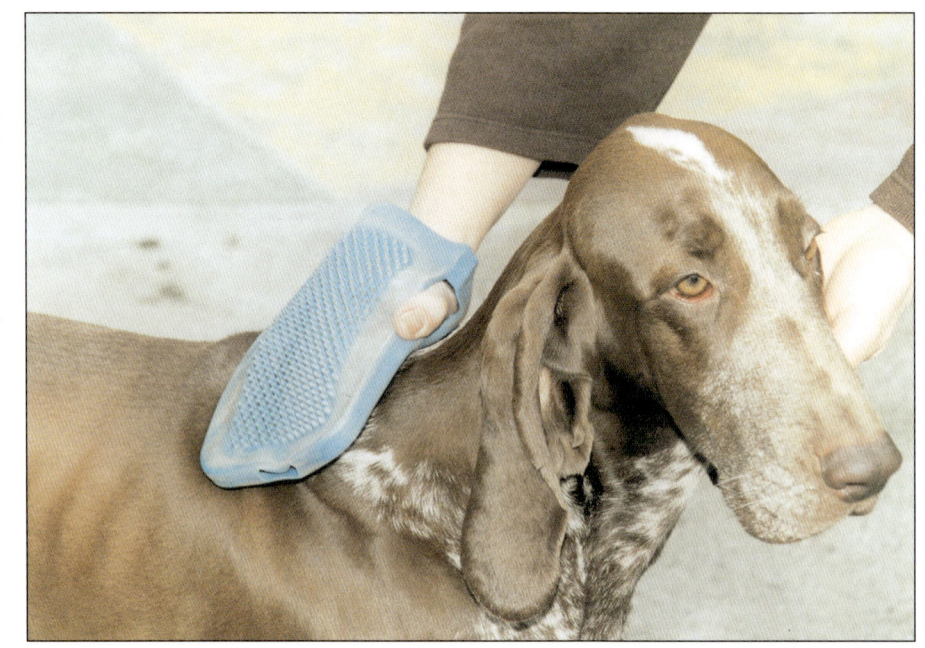

Clean the area around your dog's eyes with a soft wipe and a gentle touch.

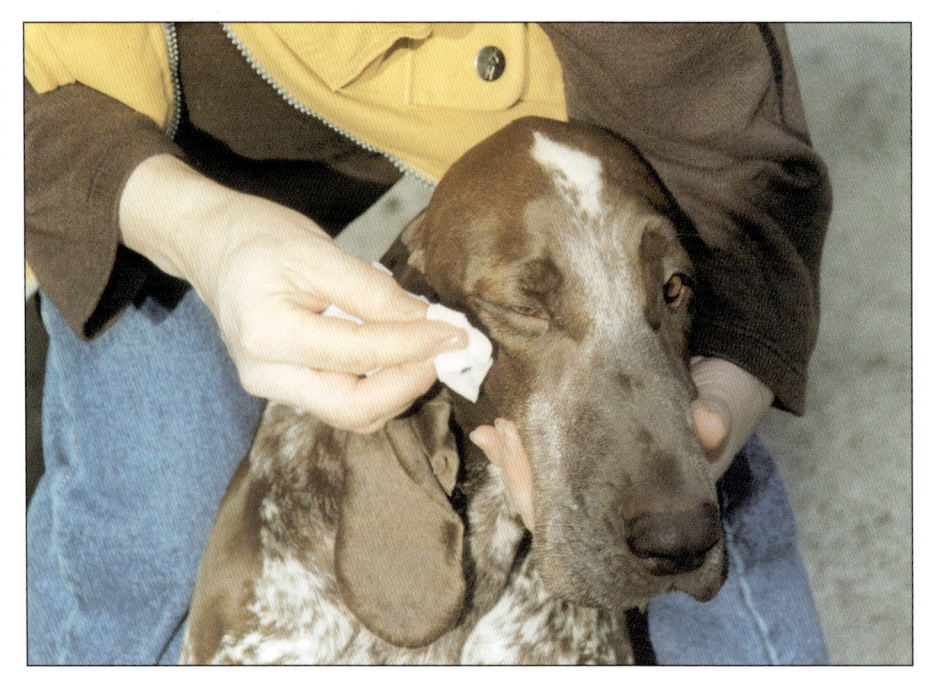

Everyday Care 71

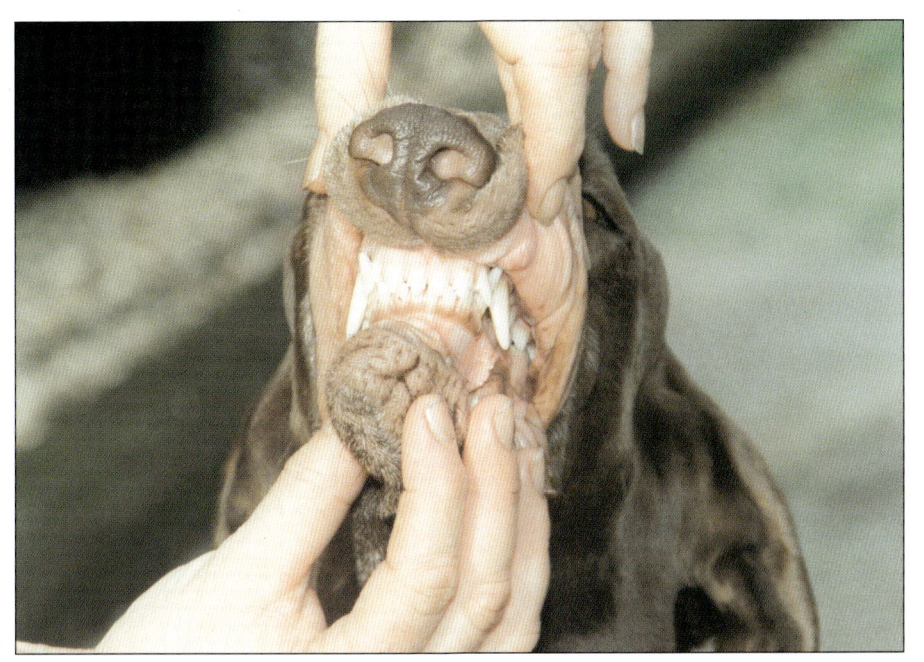

Make home dental care a part of your grooming routine to ensure that your Bracco's teeth and mouth stay healthy.

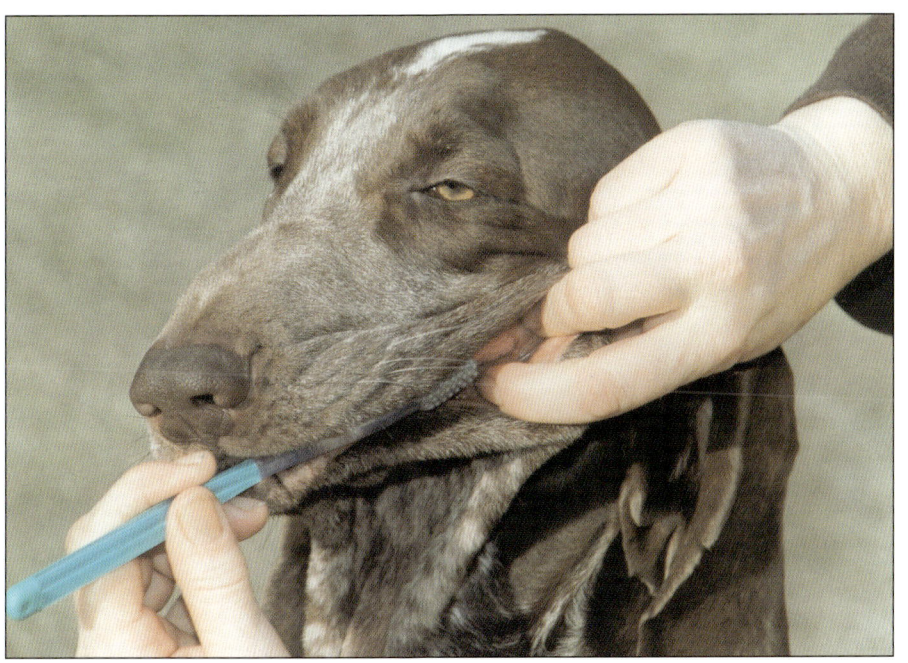

Toothbrushes and toothpaste made for dogs help to make it easy for you to maintain your dog's teeth in between veterinary visits.

Nail Clipping

Quick
Cut Line
Nail Casing

DARK-COLORED NAIL

With black or dark nails, it's best to clip only a small bit of the nail at a time or to use a file where the quick is not visible.

LIGHT-COLORED NAIL

In light-colored nails, clipping is much simpler because you can see the vein (or quick) that grows inside the nail casing.

Tooth Care

Teeth should always be kept as free from tartar as possible. There are now canine tooth-cleaning agents available, including the basics, like small toothbrushes and canine toothpaste. It is important to pay close attention to the care of teeth and gums so that they remain as healthy as possible, thereby preventing decay, infection and resultant loss.

If infection is evident in the gums, always deal with this promptly, for the infection may not just stop there. The bacteria can be carried through the bloodstream, the result of which can be disease of liver, kidney, heart and joints. This is all the more reason to realize that efficient dental care is of utmost importance throughout a dog's life, and toothbrushing can easily be implemented as a part of your regular grooming routine. Feeding dry foods is also recommended by many as a means of helping to keep teeth clean and in good condition.

Nail Clipping

Never forget that toenails should be kept short, though how frequently they will need to be clipped will depend on how much your Bracco walks on hard surfaces. Canine nail clippers can easily be obtained from pet shops, and many owners find those of the "guillotine" design easiest to use.

Everyday Care

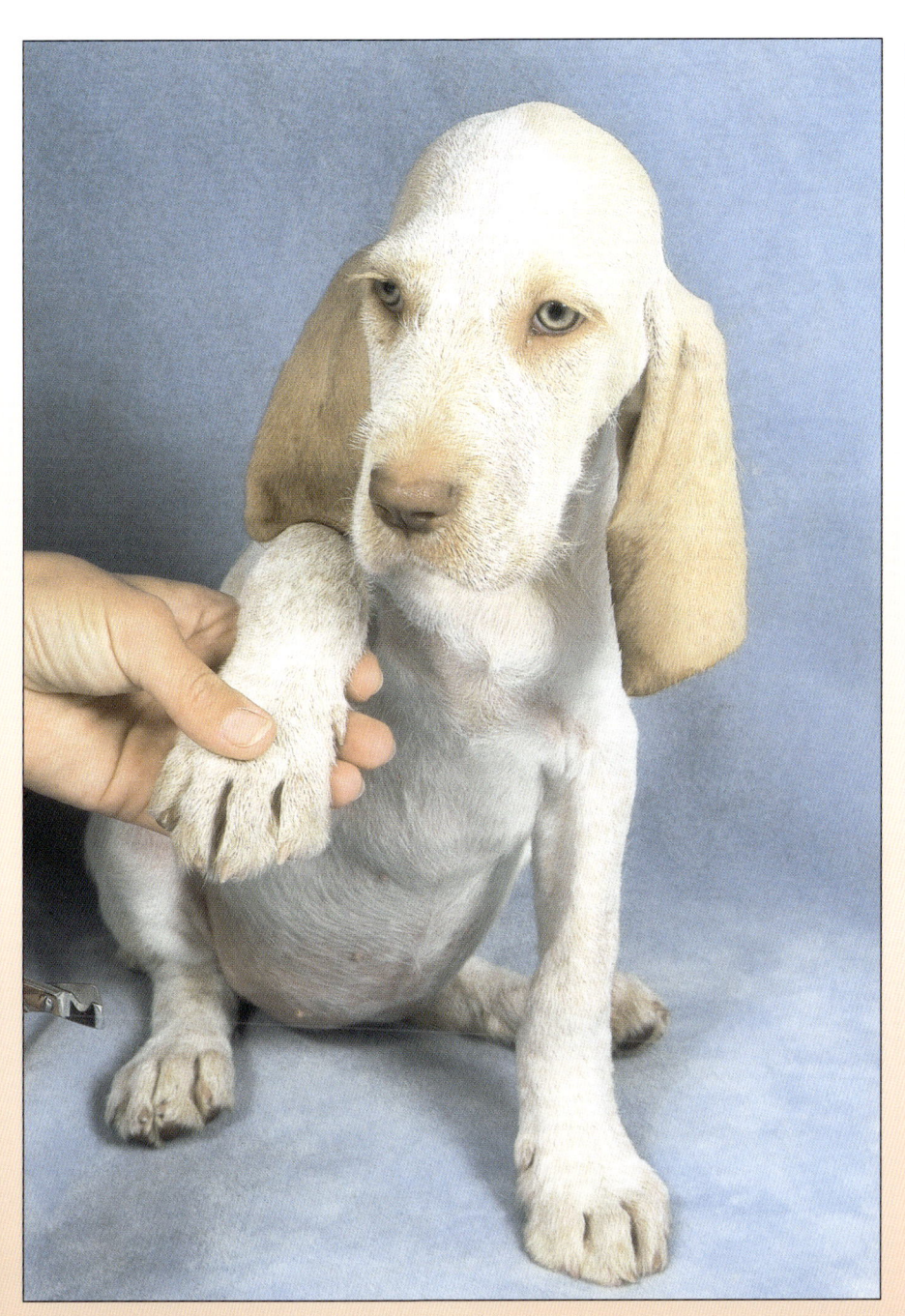

Begin the nail-trimming procedure while your Bracco is still young so that he becomes accustomed to the routine.

PEDICURE TIP
A dog that spends a lot of time outside on a hard surface, such as cement or pavement, will have his nails naturally worn down and may not need to have them trimmed as often, except maybe in the colder months when he is not outside as much. Regardless, it is best to get your dog accustomed to the nail-trimming procedure at an early age so that he is used to it. Some dogs are especially sensitive about having their feet touched, but if a dog has experienced it since puppyhood, it should not bother him.

Your Bracco should be accustomed to having his nails trimmed at an early age since nail clipping will be a part of your maintenance routine throughout his life. A dog's long nails can scratch someone unintentionally and also have a better chance of ripping and bleeding, or of causing the feet to spread. A good rule of thumb is that if you can hear your dog's nails' clicking on the floor when he walks, his nails are too long.

Before you start cutting, make sure you can identify the "quick" in each nail. The quick is a blood vessel that runs through the center of each nail and grows rather close to the end. The quick will bleed if accidentally cut, which will be quite painful for the dog as it contains nerve endings. Keep some type of clotting agent on hand, such as a styptic pencil or styptic powder (the type used for shaving). This will stop the bleeding quickly when applied to the end of the cut nail. Do not panic if you cut the quick, just stop the bleeding and talk soothingly to your dog. Once he has calmed down, move on to the next nail. It is better to clip a little at a time, particularly with black-nailed dogs.

Hold your pup steady as you begin trimming his nails; you do not want him to make any sudden movements or run away. Talk to him soothingly and stroke him as you clip. Holding his foot in your hand, simply take off the end of each nail with one swift clip.

TRAVELING WITH YOUR DOG

CAR TRAVEL
You should accustom your Bracco to riding in a car at an early age. You may or may not take him in

Everyday Care 75

the car often, but at the very least he will need to go to the vet and you do not want these trips to be traumatic for the dog or troublesome for you. The safest way for a dog to ride in the car is in his crate. If he uses a crate in the house, you can use the same crate for travel, provided your vehicle can accommodate the Bracco's large-sized crate.

Put the pup in the crate and see how he reacts. If he seems uneasy, you can have a passenger hold him on his lap while you drive. Another option for car travel is a specially made safety harness for dogs, which straps the dog in much like a seat belt. Or, if you have a station wagon, sports utility or similar large vehicle, you can partition the rear section to create a secure area for your Bracco. Do not let the dog roam loose in the vehicle—this is very dangerous! If you should stop short, your dog can be thrown and injured. If the dog starts climbing on you and pestering you while you are driving, you will not be able to concentrate on the road. It is an unsafe situation for everyone—human and canine.

For long trips, be prepared to stop to let the dog relieve himself. Take with you whatever you need

Special gates are available that fit inside many types of cars to restrain a dog safely during travel. No matter how frequently or infrequently you travel with your dog, he should never be loose in the car while you are driving.

to clean up after him, including some paper towels and old rags for use should he have a potty accident in the car or suffer from motion sickness.

AIR TRAVEL
Contact your chosen airline before proceeding with your travel plans that include your Bracco. The dog will be required to travel in a fiberglass crate and you should always check in advance with the airline regarding specific requirements for the crate's size, type and labeling. Also check with the airline's restrictions on transporting pets, as many do not do this during the summer months.

To help put the dog at ease, be sure that he is well accustomed to the crate in which he will be traveling, and give him one of his favorite toys in the crate. Do not feed the dog for several hours prior to checking in so that you minimize his need to relieve himself. Some airlines require you to provide documentation as to when the dog has last been fed. In any case, a light meal is best. For long trips, you will have to attach bowls for food and water, and a portion of food, to the outside of the dog's crate so that airline employees can tend to your Bracco between legs of the trip.

Make sure that your dog is properly identified and that your contact information appears on his ID tags and on his crate. Your Bracco will travel in a different area of the plane than the human passengers, so every rule must be strictly followed to prevent the risk of getting separated from your dog. Transporting animals is rather routine for large carriers, but you always want to play it safe.

> **TRAVEL TIP**
> When traveling, never let your dog off-lead in a strange area. Your dog could run away out of fear, decide to chase a passing squirrel or cat or simply want to stretch his legs without restriction—if any of these happen, you might never see your canine friend again.

Vacations and Boarding

So you want to take a family vacation—and you want to include *all* members of the family. You would probably make arrangements for accommodations ahead of time anyway, but this is especially important when traveling with a dog. You do not want to make an overnight stop at the only place around for miles, only to find out that the hotel does not allow dogs. Also, you do not want to reserve a place for your family without confirming that you are traveling with a dog, because, if it is against the hotel's policy, you may end up without a place to stay.

Alternatively, if you are traveling and choose not to bring your Bracco, you will have to make arrangements for him while you are away. Some options are to take him to a friend's house to stay while you are gone, to have a trusted friend stop by often or stay at your house or to bring your dog to a reputable boarding kennel. If you choose to board him at a kennel, you should visit in advance to see the facilities provided and where the dogs are kept. Are the dogs' areas spacious and kept clean? Talk to some of the employees and observe how they treat the dogs—do they spend time with the dogs, play with them, exercise them, etc.? Also find out the kennel's policy on vaccinations and what they require. This is for all of the dogs'

IDENTIFICATION OPTIONS

As puppies become more and more expensive, especially those puppies of high quality for showing and/or breeding, they have a greater chance of being stolen. The usual collar dog tag is, of course, easily removed. But there are two more permanent techniques that have become widely used for identification.

The puppy microchip implantation involves the injection of a small microchip, about the size of a corn kernel, under the skin of the dog. If your dog shows up at a clinic or shelter, or is offered for resale under less-than-savory circumstances, it can be positively identified by the microchip. The microchip is scanned, and a registry quickly identifies you as the owner.

Tattooing is done on various parts of the dog, from his belly to his ears. The number tattooed can be your telephone number, your dog's registration number or any other number that you can easily memorize. When professional dog thieves see a tattooed dog, they usually lose interest. For the safety of our dogs, no laboratory facility or dog broker will accept a tattooed dog as stock.

Discuss microchipping and tattooing with your veterinarian and breeder. Some vets perform these services on their own premises for a reasonable fee. To ensure that your dog's identification is effective, be certain that the dog is then properly registered with a legitimate national database.

BRACCO ITALIANO

> **COLLAR REQUIRED**
> If your dog gets lost, he is not able to ask for directions home. Identification tags fastened to the collar give important information—the dog's name, the owner's name, the owner's address and a telephone number where the owner can be reached. This makes it easy for whomever finds the dog to contact the owner and arrange to have the dog returned. An added advantage is that a person will be more likely to approach a lost dog who has ID tags on his collar; it tells the person that this is somebody's pet rather than a stray. This is the easiest and fastest method of identification, provided that the tags stay on the collar and the collar stays on the dog.

safety, since there is a greater risk of diseases being passed from dog to dog when dogs are kept together.

IDENTIFICATION
Your Bracco Italiano is your valued companion and friend. That is why you always keep a close eye on him and you have made sure that he cannot escape from the yard or wriggle out of his collar and run away from you. However, accidents can happen and there may come a time when your dog unexpectedly becomes separated from you. If this unfortunate event should occur, the first thing on your mind will be finding him. Proper identification, including an ID tag and possibly a tattoo and/or a microchip, will increase the chances of his being returned to you safely.

Do some research and select a suitable boarding kennel before you actually need to use it. Your vet can probably recommend a suitable kennel, or perhaps he has boarding facilities available.

Everyday Care

Your dog should always have a collar to which is attached his identification tag. A buckle collar is good for everyday use, while a more decorative collar might look nicer but not be as comfortable for frequent use.

TRAINING YOUR
BRACCO ITALIANO

Living with an untrained dog is a lot like owning a piano that you do not know how to play—it is a nice object to look at, but it does not do much more than that to bring you pleasure. Now try taking piano lessons, and suddenly the piano comes alive and brings forth magical sounds and rhythms that set your heart singing and your body swaying.

The same is true with your Bracco Italiano. Any dog is a big responsibility and, if not trained sensibly, may develop unacceptable behavior that annoys you or could even cause family friction.

To train your Bracco, you may like to enroll in an obedience class. Teach your dog good manners as you learn how and why he behaves the way he does. Find out how to communicate with your dog and how to recognize and understand his communications with you. Suddenly the dog takes on a new role in your life—he is clever, interesting, well behaved and fun to be with. He demonstrates his bond of devotion to you daily. In other words, your Bracco does wonders for your ego

Puppies seem to operate at either "stop" or "go"— their bursts of activity are punctuated by frequent naps and rest periods.

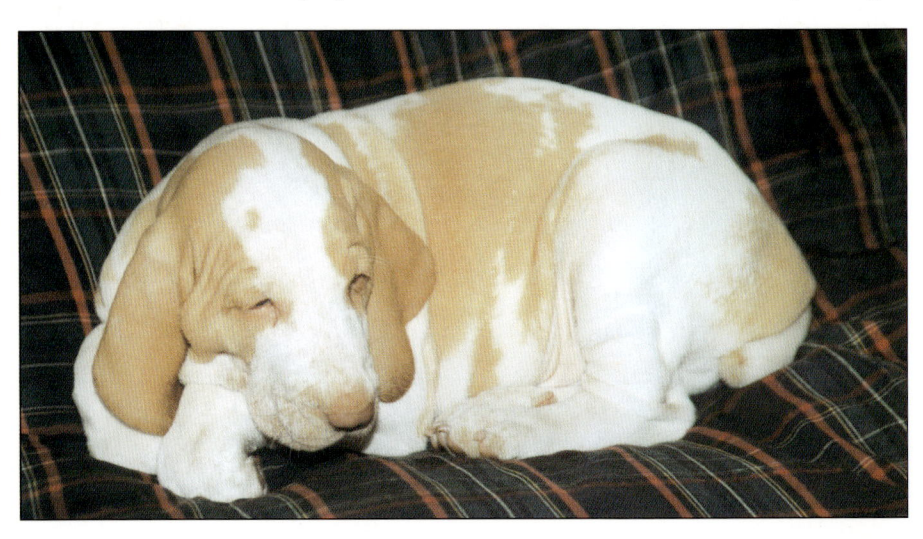

because he constantly reminds you that you are not only his leader, you are his hero!

Those involved with teaching dog obedience and counseling owners about their dogs' behavior have discovered some interesting facts about dog ownership. For example, training dogs when they are puppies results in the highest rate of success in developing well-mannered and well-adjusted adult dogs. Training an older dog, from six months to six years of age, can produce almost equal results, providing that the owner accepts the dog's slower rate of learning capability and is willing to work patiently to help the dog succeed at developing to his fullest potential. Unfortunately, many owners of untrained adult dogs lack the patience factor, so they do not persist until their dogs are successful at learning particular behaviors.

Training a puppy aged 10 to 16 weeks (20 weeks at the most) is like working with a dry sponge in a pool of water. The pup soaks up whatever you show him and constantly looks for more things to do and learn. At this early age, his body is not yet producing hormones, and therein lies the reason for such a high rate of success. Without hormones, the pup is focused on his owners and not particularly interested in investigating other places, dogs, people, etc. You are his leader: his

REAP THE REWARDS
If you start with a normal, healthy dog and give him time, patience and some carefully executed lessons, you will reap the rewards of that training for the life of the dog. And what a life it will be! The two of you will find immeasurable pleasure in the companionship you have built together with love, respect and understanding.

Your Bracco puppy needs your guidance. At this young age, he's just waiting to soak up the lessons that you teach him.

provider of food, water, shelter and security. He latches onto you and wants to stay close. He will usually follow you from room to room, will not let you out of his sight when you are outdoors with him and will respond in like manner to the people and animals you encounter. If you greet a friend warmly, he will be happy to greet the person as well. If, however, you are hesitant or anxious about the approach of a stranger, he will respond accordingly.

Once the puppy begins to produce hormones, his natural curiosity emerges and he begins to investigate the world around him. It is at this time when you may notice that the untrained dog begins to wander away from you and even ignore your commands to stay close. When this behavior becomes a problem, you have two choices: get rid of the dog or train him. It is strongly urged that you choose the latter option.

You usually will be able to find obedience classes within a reasonable distance from your home, but you can also do a lot to train your dog yourself. Sometimes there are classes available, but the tuition is too costly. Whatever the circumstances, the solution to training your dog without formal obedience classes lies within the pages of this book. This chapter is devoted to helping you train your Bracco Italiano at home. If the recommended procedures are followed faithfully, you may expect positive results that will prove rewarding both to you and your dog.

Whether your new charge is a puppy or a mature adult, the methods of teaching and the techniques we use in training basic behaviors are the same. After all, no dog, whether puppy or adult, likes harsh or inhumane methods;

CALM DOWN

Dogs will do anything for your attention. If you reward the dog when he is calm and attentive, you will develop a well-mannered dog. If, on the other hand, you greet your dog excitedly and encourage him to wrestle with you, the dog will greet you the same way and you will have a hyperactive dog on your hands.

this is particularly true of the sensitive Bracco. You will get nowhere using negative training methods with this breed. All creatures, however, respond favorably to gentle motivational methods and sincere praise and encouragement. Now let us get started.

HOUSE-TRAINING

You can train a puppy to relieve himself wherever you choose, but this must be somewhere suitable. You should bear in mind from the outset that when your puppy is old enough to go out in public places, any canine droppings must be removed at once. You will always have to carry with you a small plastic bag or "poop-scoop."

Outdoor training includes such surfaces as grass, soil and cement. Indoor training usually means training your dog to newspaper, although this is usually not a viable option for owners of large dogs like the Bracco. When deciding on the surface and location that you will want your Bracco to use, be sure it is going to be permanent. Training your dog to grass and then changing your mind a few months later is extremely difficult for both dog and owner.

Next, choose the command you will use each and every time you want your puppy to void. "Hurry up" and "Potty" are examples of commands commonly

PARENTAL GUIDANCE
Training a dog is a life experience. Many parents admit that much of what they know about raising children they learned from caring for their dogs. Dogs respond to love, fairness and guidance, just as children do. Become a good dog owner and you may become an even better parent.

CANINE DEVELOPMENT SCHEDULE

It is important to understand how and at what age a puppy develops into adulthood. If you are a puppy owner, consult the following Canine Development Schedule to determine the stage of development your puppy is currently experiencing. This knowledge will help you as you work with the puppy in the weeks and months ahead.

Period	Age	Characteristics
First to Third	Birth to Seven Weeks	Puppy needs food, sleep and warmth, and responds to simple and gentle touching. Needs mother for security and disciplining. Needs littermates for learning and interacting with other dogs. Pup learns to function within a pack and learns pack order of dominance. Begin socializing pup with adults and children for short periods. Pup begins to become aware of his environment.
Fourth	Eight to Twelve Weeks	Brain is fully developed. Needs socializing with outside world. Remove from mother and littermates. Needs to change from canine pack to human pack. Human dominance necessary. Fear period occurs between 8 and 12 weeks. Avoid fright and pain.
Fifth	Thirteen to Sixteen Weeks	Training and formal obedience should begin. Less association with other dogs, more with people, places, situations. Period will pass easily if you remember this is pup's change-to-adolescence time. Be firm and fair. Flight instinct prominent. Permissiveness and over-disciplining can do permanent damage. Praise for good behavior.
Juvenile	Four to Eight Months	Another fear period about 7 to 8 months of age. It passes quickly, but be cautious of fright and pain. Sexual maturity reached. Dominant traits established. Dog should understand sit, down, come and stay by now.

NOTE: THESE ARE APPROXIMATE TIME FRAMES. ALLOW FOR INDIVIDUAL DIFFERENCES IN PUPPIES.

Training

SAFETY FIRST

While it may seem that the most important things to your dog are eating, sleeping and chewing the upholstery on your furniture, his first concern is actually safety. The domesticated dogs we keep as companions have the same pack instinct as their ancestors who ran free thousands of years ago. Because of this pack instinct, your dog wants to know that he and his pack are not in danger of being harmed, and that his pack has a strong, capable leader. You must establish yourself as the leader early on in your relationship. That way your dog will trust that you will take care of him and the pack, and he will accept your commands without question.

used by dog owners. Get in the habit of giving the puppy your chosen relief command before you take him out. That way, when he becomes an adult, you will be able to determine if he wants to go out when you ask him. A confirmation will be signs of interest, such as wagging his tail, watching you intently, going to the door, etc.

Puppy's Needs

Puppy needs to relieve himself after play periods, after each meal, after he has been sleeping and at any time he indicates that he is looking for a place to urinate or defecate. The urinary and intestinal tract muscles of very young puppies are not fully developed. Therefore, like human babies, puppies need to relieve themselves frequently.

Take your puppy out often—every hour for an eight-week-old, for example—and always immediately after sleeping and eating. The older the puppy, the less often he will need to relieve himself. Finally, as a mature healthy adult, he will require only three to five relief trips per day.

Housing

Since the types of housing and control you provide for your puppy have a direct relationship on the success of house-training, we consider the various aspects of both before we begin training.

Taking a new puppy home and turning him loose in your house can be compared to turning a child loose in an amusement

The breeder starts early training with the young pups on newspaper, but you'll change to outdoor training once your Bracco comes home with you.

park and telling the child that the place is all his! The sheer enormity of the place would be too much for him to handle. Instead, offer the puppy clearly defined areas where he can play, sleep, eat and live. A room of the house where the family gathers is the most obvious choice. Puppies are social animals and need to feel a part of the pack right from the start. Hearing your voice, watching you while you are doing things and smelling you nearby are all positive reinforcers that he

The pup will learn to locate his relief area using his scenting ability. Soon he will learn to go there on his own.

> **THINK BEFORE YOU BARK**
> Dogs are sensitive to their masters' moods and emotions. Use your voice wisely when communicating with your dog. Never raise your voice at your dog unless you are trying to correct him. "Barking" at your dog can become as meaningless as "dogspeak" is to you.

is now a member of your pack. Usually a family room, the kitchen or a nearby adjoining breakfast area is ideal for providing safety and security for both puppy and owner.

Within the designated room, there should be a smaller area that the puppy can call his own. An alcove, a wire or fiberglass dog crate or a partitioned (not boarded!) corner from which he can view the activities of his new family will be fine. The size of the area or crate is the key factor here. The area must be large enough so that the puppy can lie down and stretch out, as well as stand up, without rubbing his head on the top. At the same time, it must be small enough so that he cannot relieve himself at one end and sleep at the other without coming into contact with his droppings. Dogs are, by nature, clean animals and will not remain close to their relief areas unless forced to do so. In those cases, they then become dirty dogs and usually remain that way for life.

The dog's designated area should contain clean bedding and a toy. Before house-training is complete, avoid putting food or water in the dog's crate. Eating and drinking will stimulate the dog's digestive (and thus elimination) processes, which will defeat your purpose in training as well as make the puppy very uncomfortable as he tries to "hold it." Once house-training is accomplished, water must always be available, in a non-spill container.

CONTROL
By control, we mean helping the puppy to create a lifestyle pattern that will be compatible to that of his human pack (you!). Just as we guide little children to learn our way of life, we must show the puppy when it is time to play, eat, sleep, exercise and even entertain himself.

Your puppy should always sleep in his crate. He should also learn that, during times of household confusion and excessive human activity, such as at breakfast when family members are preparing for the day, he can play by himself in relative safety and comfort in his designated area. Each time you leave the puppy alone, he should understand exactly where he is to stay.

Puppies are chewers and cannot tell the difference between things like lamp cords, television wires, shoes, table legs, etc.

HOW MANY TIMES A DAY?

AGE	RELIEF TRIPS
To 14 weeks	10
14–22 weeks	8
22–32 weeks	6
Adulthood (dog stops growing)	4

These are estimates, of course, but they are a guide to the *minimum* number of opportunities a dog should have each day to relieve himself.

Chewing into a television wire, for example, can be fatal to the puppy, while a shorted wire can start a fire in the house. If the puppy chews on the arm of the chair when he is alone, you will probably discipline him angrily when you get home. Thus, he makes the association that your coming home means he is going to be punished. (He will not remember chewing the chair and is incapable of making the association of the discipline with his naughty deed.) Accustoming the pup to his designated area not only keeps him safe but also avoids his engaging in destructive behaviors when you are not around.

Times of excitement, such as special occasions, family parties, etc., can be fun for the puppy, providing that he can view the activities from the security of his designated area. He is not under-

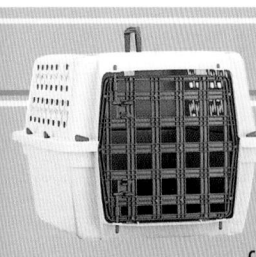

THE SUCCESS METHOD

Success that comes by luck is usually short-lived. Success that comes by well-thought-out proven methods is often more easily achieved and permanent. This is the Success Method. It is designed to give you, the puppy owner, a simple yet proven way to help your puppy develop clean living habits and a feeling of security in his new environment.

6 Steps to Successful Crate Training

1 Tell the puppy "Crate time!" and place him in the crate with a small treat (a piece of cheese or half of a biscuit). Let him stay in the crate for five minutes while you are in the same room. Then release him and praise lavishly. Never release him when he is fussing. Wait until he is quiet before you let him out.

2 Repeat Step 1 several times a day.

3 The next day, place the puppy in the crate as before. Let him stay there for ten minutes. Do this several times.

4 Continue building time in five-minute increments until the puppy stays in his crate for 30 minutes with you in the room. Always take him to his relief area after prolonged periods in his crate.

5 Now go back to Step 1 and let the puppy stay in his crate for five minutes, this time while you are out of the room.

6 Once again, build crate time in five-minute increments with you out of the room. When the puppy will stay willingly in his crate (he may even fall asleep!) for 30 minutes with you out of the room, he will be ready to stay in it for several hours at a time.

foot and he is not being fed all sorts of tidbits that will probably cause him stomach distress, yet he still feels a part of the fun.

Establishing a Schedule

A puppy should be taken to his relief area each time he is released from his designated area, after meals, after play sessions and when he first awakens in the morning (at age eight weeks, this can mean 5 a.m.!). The puppy will indicate that he's ready "to go" by circling or sniffing busily—do not misinterpret these signs. For a puppy less than ten weeks of age, a routine of taking him out every hour is necessary. As the puppy grows, he will be able to wait for longer periods of time.

Keep trips to his relief area short. Stay no more than five or six minutes and then return to the house. If he goes during that time, praise him lavishly and take him indoors immediately. If he does not, but he has an accident when you go back indoors, pick him up immediately, say "No! No!" and return to his relief area. Wait a few minutes, then return to the house again. Never hit a puppy or put his face in urine or excrement when he has had an accident!

Once indoors, put the puppy in his crate until you have had time to clean up his accident. Then, release him to the family area and watch him more closely than before. Chances are, his accident was a result of your not picking up his signal or waiting too long before offering him the opportunity to relieve himself. Never hold a grudge against the puppy for accidents.

Let the puppy learn that going outdoors means it is time to

HOUSE-TRAINING TIP

Most of all, be consistent. Always take your dog to the same location, always use the same command and always have the dog on lead when he is in his relief area, unless a fenced-in yard is available.

By following the Success Method, your puppy will be completely house-broken by the time his muscle and brain development reach maturity. Keep in mind that small breeds usually mature faster than large breeds, but all puppies should be trained by six months of age.

> **TAKE THE LEAD**
> Do not carry your dog to his relief area. Lead him there on a leash or, better yet, encourage him to follow you to the spot. If you start carrying him to his spot, you might end up doing this routine forever and your dog will have the satisfaction of having trained *you*.

command, whatever suits best. Soon he will run to his crate or special area when he hears you say those words. Crate training provides safety for you, the puppy and the home. It also provides the puppy with a feeling of security, and that helps the puppy achieve self-confidence and clean habits. Remember that one of the primary ingredients in house-training your puppy is control. Regardless of your lifestyle, there will always be occasions when you will need to have a place where your dog can stay and be happy and safe. Crate training is the answer for now and in the future.

In conclusion, a few key elements are really all you need for a successful house-training method—consistency, frequency, praise, control and supervision. By following these procedures with a normal, healthy puppy, you and the puppy will soon be past the stage of accidents and ready to move on to a clean and rewarding life together.

ROLES OF DISCIPLINE, REWARD AND PUNISHMENT

Discipline, training one to act in accordance with rules, brings order to life. It is as simple as that. Without discipline, particularly in a group society, chaos will reign supreme and the group will eventually perish. Humans and canines are social animals and need some form of discipline in

relieve himself, not to play. Once trained, he will be able to play indoors and out and still differentiate between the times for play versus the times for relief. Help him develop regular hours for naps, being alone, playing by himself and just resting, all in his crate. Encourage him to entertain himself while you are busy with your activities. Let him learn that having you near is comforting, but it is not your main purpose in life to provide him with undivided attention.

Each time you put your puppy in his own area, use the same

order to function effectively. They must procure food, reproduce to keep their species going and protect their home base and their young. If there were no discipline in the lives of social animals, they would eventually die from starvation and/or predation by other stronger animals. In the case of domestic canines, discipline in their lives is needed in order for them to understand how their pack (you and other family members) functions and how they must act in order to survive.

A large humane society in a highly populated area recently surveyed dog owners regarding their satisfaction with their relationships with their dogs. People who had trained their dogs were 75% more satisfied with their pets than those who had never trained their dogs.

Dr. Edward Thorndike, a noted psychologist, established *Thorndike's Theory of Learning*, which states that a behavior that results in a pleasant event tends to be repeated. Furthermore, it concludes that a behavior that results in an unpleasant event tends not to be repeated. It is this theory upon which training methods are based today, and you will focus on positive reinforcement when training your Bracco. For example, if you manipulate a dog to perform a specific behavior and reward him for doing it, he is likely to do it again because he enjoyed the end result.

Occasionally, punishment, a penalty inflicted for an offense, is necessary. The best type of punishment often comes from an outside source. For example, a child is told not to touch the stove because he may get burned. He disobeys and touches the stove. In doing so, he receives a burn. From that time on, he respects the heat of the stove and avoids contact with it. Therefore, a behavior that results in an unpleasant event tends not to be repeated.

A good example of a dog's learning the hard way is the dog who chases the house cat. He is told many times to leave the cat alone, yet he persists in teasing the cat. Then, one day, the dog begins chasing the cat but the cat turns and swipes a claw across the dog's face, leaving the dog with a painful gash on his nose. The final result is that the dog stops chasing the cat.

> **TRAINING RULES**
> If you want to be successful in training your dog, you have four rules to obey yourself:
> 1. Develop an understanding of how a dog thinks.
> 2. Do not blame the dog for lack of communication.
> 3. Define your dog's personality and act accordingly.
> 4. Have patience and be consistent.

TRAINING EQUIPMENT

Collar and Lead
For a Bracco Italiano, the collar and lead that you use for training must be one with which you are easily able to work, not too heavy for the dog and perfectly safe.

Treats
Have a bag of treats on hand; something nutritious and easy to swallow works best. Use a soft treat, a chunk of cheese or a piece of cooked chicken rather than a dry biscuit. By the time the dog has finished chewing a dry treat, he will forget why he is being rewarded in the first place!

Incidentally, using food rewards will not teach a dog to beg at the table—the only way to teach a dog to beg at the table is to give him food from the table. In training, rewarding the dog with a food treat will help him associate praise and the treats with learning new behaviors that obviously please his owner.

TRAINING BEGINS: ASK THE DOG A QUESTION
In order to teach your dog anything, you must first get his attention. After all, he cannot learn anything if he is looking away from you with his mind on something else. To get your dog's attention, ask him "School?" and immediately walk over to him and give him a treat as you tell

> **THE GOLDEN RULE**
> The golden rule of dog training is simple. For each "question" (command), there is only one correct answer (reaction). One command = one reaction. Keep practicing the command until the dog reacts correctly without hesitating. Be repetitive but not monotonous. Dogs get bored just as people do!

him "Good dog." Wait a minute or two and repeat the routine, this time with a treat in your hand as you approach within a foot of the dog. Do not go directly to him, but stop about a foot short of him and hold out the treat as you ask "School?" He will see you approaching with a treat in your hand and most likely begin walking toward you. As you meet, give him the treat and praise again.

The third time, ask the question, have a treat in your hand and walk only a short distance toward the dog so that he must walk almost all the way to you. As he reaches you, give him the treat and praise again. By this time, the dog will probably be getting the idea that if he pays attention to you, especially when you ask that question, it will pay off in treats and enjoyable activities for him. In other words, he learns that "school" means doing great things with you that are fun

Training

PRACTICE MAKES PERFECT!
- Have training lessons with your dog every day in several short segments—three to five times a day for a few minutes at a time is ideal.
- Do not have long practice sessions. The dog will become easily bored.
- Never practice when you are tired, ill, worried or in an otherwise negative mood. This will transmit to the dog and may have an adverse effect on his performance.

Think fun, short and above all *positive!* End each session on a high note, rather than a failed exercise, and make sure to give a lot of praise. Enjoy the training and help your dog enjoy it, too.

and that result in positive attention for him.

Remember that the dog does not understand your verbal language; he only recognizes sounds. Your question translates to a series of sounds for him, and those sounds become the signal to go to you and pay attention. The dog learns that if he does this, he will get to interact with you plus receive treats and praise.

THE BASIC COMMANDS

TEACHING SIT
Now that you have the dog's attention, attach his lead and hold it in your left hand, and hold a food treat in your right hand. Place your food hand at the dog's nose and let him lick the treat but not take it from you. Say "Sit" and slowly raise your food hand from in front of the dog's nose up over his head so that he is looking at the ceiling. As he bends his head upward, he will have to bend his knees to maintain his balance. As he bends his knees, he will assume a sit position. At that point, release the food treat and praise lavishly with comments such as "Good dog! Good sit!," etc. Remember to always praise enthusiastically, because dogs relish verbal praise from their owners and feel so proud of themselves whenever they accomplish a behavior.

You will not use food forever in getting the dog to obey your commands. Food is only used to teach new behaviors and, once the dog knows what you want when you give a specific command, you will wean him off the food treats but still maintain

Your puppy may fidget and squirm while he's getting used to his collar and leash, but soon he will not even notice that he's wearing it.

Praise your puppy with "Good sit" whenever he assumes the sit position—whether during training or not. He will learn to associate the word "sit" with his action and learn the command more easily.

Training

the verbal praise. After all, you will always have your voice with you, and there will be many times when you have no food rewards but expect the dog to obey.

TEACHING DOWN

Teaching the down exercise is easy when you understand how the dog perceives the down position, and it is very difficult when you do not. Dogs perceive the down position as a submissive one; therefore, teaching the down exercise by using a forceful method can sometimes make the dog develop such a fear of the down that he either runs away when you say "Down" or he attempts to snap at the person who tries to force him down.

Have the dog sit close alongside your left leg, facing in the same direction as you are. Hold the lead in your left hand and a food treat in your right. Now place your left hand lightly on the top of the dog's shoulders where they meet above the spinal cord. Do not push down on the dog's shoulders; simply rest your left hand there so you can guide the dog to lie down close to your left leg rather than to swing away from your side when he drops.

Now place the food hand at the dog's nose, say "Down" very softly (almost a whisper) and slowly lower the food hand to the dog's front feet. When the food hand reaches the floor, begin moving it forward along the floor in front of the dog. Keep talking softly to the dog, saying things like, "Do you want this treat? You can do this, good dog." Your reassuring tone of voice will help calm the dog as he tries to follow the food hand in order to get the treat.

When the dog's elbows touch the floor, release the food and praise softly. Try to get the dog to maintain that down position for several seconds before you let him sit up again. The goal here is to

> **DOUBLE JEOPARDY**
> A dog in jeopardy never lies down. He stays alert on his feet because instinct tells him that he may have to run away or fight for his survival. Therefore, if a dog feels threatened or anxious, he will not lie down. Consequently, it is important to keep the dog calm and relaxed as he learns the down exercise.

get the dog to settle down and not feel threatened in the down position.

Teaching Stay

It is easy to teach the dog to stay in either a sit or a down position. Again, we use food and praise during the teaching process as we

> **COMMAND STANCE**
> Stand up straight and authoritatively when giving your dog commands. Do not issue commands when lying on the floor or lying on your back on the sofa. If you are on your hands and knees when you give a command, your dog will think you are positioning yourself to play.

Right: Have the dog facing you in the sit position, and make sure his attention is focused on you as you give the stay command and hand signal.
Below: Using the same verbal command and hand signal, increase the distance as the dog learns to stay.

help the dog to understand exactly what it is that we are expecting him to do.

To teach the sit/stay, start with the dog sitting on your left side as before and hold the lead in your left hand. Have a food treat in your right hand and place your food hand at the dog's nose. Say "Stay" and step out on your right foot to stand directly in front of the dog, toe to toe, as he licks and nibbles the treat. Be sure to keep his head facing upward to maintain the sit position. Count to five and then swing around to stand next to the dog again with him on your left. As soon as you get back to the original position, release the food and praise lavishly.

To teach the down/stay, do the down as previously described. As soon as the dog lies down, say "Stay" and step out on your right foot just as you did in the sit/stay. Count to five and then return to stand beside the dog with him on your left side. Release the treat and praise as always.

Training

Within a week or ten days, you can begin to add a bit of distance between you and your dog when you leave him. When you do, use your left hand open with the palm facing the dog as a stay signal, much the same as the hand signal a police officer uses to stop traffic at an intersection. Hold the food treat in your right hand as before, but this time the food will not be touching the dog's nose. He will watch the food hand and quickly learn that he is going to get that treat as soon as you return to his side.

When you can stand 3 feet away from your dog for 30 seconds, you can then begin building time and distance in both stays. Eventually, the dog can be expected to remain in the stay position for prolonged periods of time until you return to him or call him to you. Always praise lavishly when he stays.

TEACHING COME

If you make teaching "come" an exciting experience, you should never have a student that does not love the game or that fails to come when called. The secret, it seems, is never to teach the word "come."

At times when an owner most wants his dog to come when called, the owner is likely to be upset or anxious and he allows these feelings to come through in the tone of his voice when he calls his dog. Hearing that desperation in his owner's voice, the dog fears the results of going to him and therefore either disobeys outright or runs in the opposite direction. The secret, therefore, is to teach the dog a game and, when you want him to come to you, simply play the game. It is practically a no-fail solution!

To begin, have several members of your family take a few food treats and each go into a different room in the house. Everyone takes turns calling the dog, and each person should cele-

"WHERE ARE YOU?"

When calling the dog, do not say "Come." Say things like, "Rover, where are you? See if you can find me! I have a biscuit for you!" Keep up a constant line of chatter with coaxing sounds and frequent questions such as "Where are you?" The dog will learn to follow the sound of your voice to locate you and receive his reward.

Your Bracco should be eager to come running when he hears you call!

brate the dog's finding him with a treat and lots of happy praise. When a person calls the dog, he is actually inviting the dog to find him and to get a treat as a reward for "winning." A few turns of the "Where are you?" game and the dog will understand that everyone is playing the game and that each person has a big celebration awaiting the dog's success at locating him or her. Once the dog learns to love the game, simply calling out "Where are you?" will bring him running from wherever he is when he hears that all-important question.

The come command is recognized as one of the most important things to teach a dog, but there are trainers who work with thousands of dogs and never use the actual word "come." Yet these dogs will race to respond to a person who uses the dog's name followed by "Where are you?" For example, a woman has a 12-year-old companion dog who went blind, but who never fails to locate her owner when asked, "Where are you?"

Children, in particular, love to play this game with their dogs. Children can hide in smaller places like a shower stall or bathtub, behind a bed or under a table. The dog needs to work a little bit harder to find these hiding places, but, when he does, he loves to celebrate with a treat and a tussle with a favorite youngster.

TEACHING HEEL

Heeling means that the dog walks beside the owner without pulling. It takes time and patience on the owner's part to succeed at teaching the dog that he (the owner) will not proceed unless the dog is walking calmly beside him. Neither pulling out ahead on the lead nor lagging behind is acceptable on-lead behavior.

Begin by holding the lead in your left hand as the dog sits beside your left leg. Move the loop end of the lead to your right

---

"COME"...BACK

Never call your dog to come to you for a correction or scold him when he reaches you. That is the quickest way to turn a come command into "Go away fast!" Dogs think only in the present tense, and your dog will connect the scolding with coming to you, not with the misbehavior of a few moments earlier.

hand, but keep your left hand short on the lead so that it keeps the dog in close next to you. Say "Heel" and step forward on your left foot. Keep the dog close to you and take three steps. Stop and have the dog sit next to you in what we now call the heel position. Praise verbally, but do not touch the dog. Hesitate a moment and begin again with "Heel," taking three steps and stopping, at which point the dog is told to sit again.

Your goal here is to have the dog walk those three steps without pulling on the lead. Once he will walk calmly beside you for three steps without pulling, increase the number of steps you take to five. When he will walk politely beside you while you take five steps, you can increase the length of your walk to ten steps. Keep increasing the length of your stroll until the dog will walk quietly beside you without pulling as long as you want him to heel. When you stop heeling, indicate to the dog that the exercise is over by verbally praising as you pet him and say "OK, good dog." The "OK" is used as a release word, meaning that the exercise is finished and the dog is free to relax.

If you are dealing with a dog who insists on pulling you around, simply "put on your brakes" and stand your ground until the dog realizes that the two of you are not going anywhere until he is beside you and moving at your pace, not his. It may take some time just standing there to convince the dog that you are the leader and that you will be the one to decide on the direction and speed of your travel.

TUG OF WALK?
If you begin teaching the heel by taking long walks and letting the dog pull you along, he misinterprets this action as an acceptable form of taking a walk. When you pull back on the leash to counteract his pulling, he reads that tug as a signal to pull even harder! Be consistent in encouraging your Bracco's polite behavior on lead.

The heel command is used in the show ring, as the dogs must behave politely on lead while the judge evaluates their movement.

Each time the dog looks up at you or slows down to give a slack lead between the two of you, quietly praise him and say, "Good heel. Good dog." Eventually, the dog will begin to respond and within a few days he will be walking politely beside you without pulling on the lead. At first, the training sessions should be kept short and very positive; soon the dog will be able to walk nicely with you for increasingly longer distances. Remember also to give the dog free time and the opportunity to run and play when you have finished heel practice.

WEANING OFF FOOD IN TRAINING

Food is used in training new behaviors. Once the dog understands what behavior goes with a specific command, it is time to start weaning him off the food treats. At first, give a treat after each exercise. Then, start to give a treat only after every other exercise. Mix up the times when you offer a food reward and the times when you offer only praise so that the dog will never know when he is going to receive both food and praise and when he is going to receive only praise. This is called a variable-ratio reward system. It proves successful because there is always the chance that the owner will produce a treat, so the dog never stops trying for that reward. No matter what, *always* give verbal praise.

OBEDIENCE CLASSES

It is a good idea to enroll in an obedience class if one is available in your area. If yours is a show dog, handling classes to prepare the two of you for the ring would be more appropriate. Many areas

> ### HEELING WELL
> Teach your dog to heel in an enclosed area. Once you think the dog will obey reliably and you want to attempt advanced obedience exercises such as off-lead heeling, test him in a fenced-in area so he cannot run away.

have dog clubs that offer basic obedience training as well as preparatory classes for obedience competition. There are also local dog trainers who offer similar classes.

At obedience shows and trials, dogs can earn titles at various levels of competition. The beginning levels of obedience competition include basic behaviors such as sit, down, heel, etc. The more advanced levels of competition include jumping, retrieving, scent discrimination and signal work. The advanced levels require a dog and owner to put a lot of time and effort into their training. The titles that can be earned at these levels of competition are very prestigious.

OTHER ACTIVITIES FOR LIFE

Whether a dog is trained in the structured environment of a class or alone with his owner at home, there are many activities that can bring fun and rewards to both owner and dog once they have mastered basic control. Teaching the dog to help out around the home, in the yard or on the farm provides great satisfaction to both dog and owner. In addition, the dog's help makes life a little easier for his owner and raises the dog's stature as a valued companion to his family. It helps give the dog a purpose by occupying his mind and providing an outlet for his energy. To expand his helping

> **HOW TO WEAN THE "TREAT HOG"**
> If you have trained your dog by rewarding him with a treat each time he performs a command, he may soon decide that without the treat, he won't sit, stay or come. The best way to fix this problem is to start asking your dog to do certain commands twice before being rewarded. Slowly increase the number of commands given and then vary the number: three sits and a treat one day, five sits for a biscuit the next day, etc. Your dog will soon realize that there is no set number of sits before he gets his reward and he'll likely do it the first time you ask in the hope of being rewarded sooner rather than later.

paws outside the home, contact a therapy-dog organization, as some Bracchi have shown a real aptitude for therapy work.

Backpacking is an exciting and healthy activity that the dog can be taught without assistance from more than his owner. The exercise of walking and climbing is good for man and dog alike, and the bond that they develop together is priceless. The rule for backpacking with any dog is never to expect the dog to carry more than one-sixth of his body weight.

If you are interested in participating in organized competition with your Bracco, there are activities other than obedience in which you and your dog can become involved. Of course, as a hunt, point and retrieve breed, the Bracco excels in field trials and hunting events, as these allow the dog to explore and develop his innate talents. Bracchi also possess excellent scenting ability, which make them naturals at tracking events. Agility is a popular sport in which dogs run through obstacle courses that include various jumps, tunnels and other exercises to test the dog's speed and coordination. The owners run beside their dogs to give commands and to guide them through the course. Although competitive, the focus is on fun—it's fun to do, fun to watch and great exercise.

Dog showing is an exciting activity for you and your Bracco, with the added benefit of meeting people and making friends who share your interest in the breed.

Training 103

A Bracco puppy is introduced to a bird's wing to stimulate his natural instincts as a precursor to formal hunting training.

An adult Bracco retrieving a rabbit. This breed excels in the field with the hunter as well as in competitive field and hunting events.

PHYSICAL STRUCTURE OF THE BRACCO ITALIANO

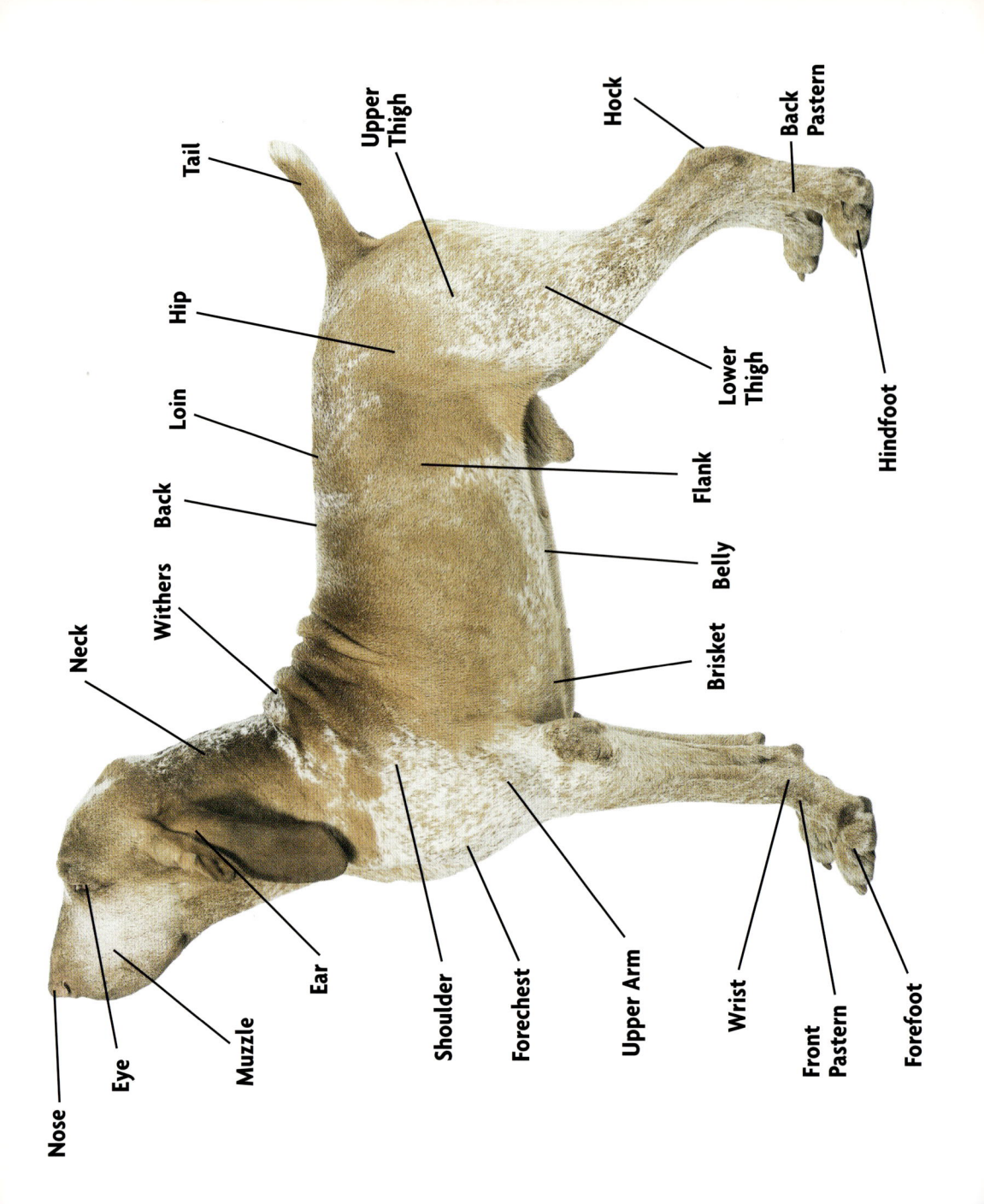

HEALTH CARE OF YOUR
BRACCO ITALIANO

Dogs suffer from many of the same physical illnesses as people and might even share many of the same psychological problems. Since people usually know more about human diseases than canine maladies, many of the terms used in this chapter will be familiar but not necessarily those used by vets. For example, we will use the familiar term *x-ray* instead of *radiograph*. We will also use the familiar term *symptoms*, even though dogs don't have symptoms, which are verbal descriptions of something the patient feels or observes himself that he regards as abnormal. Dogs have *clinical signs* since they cannot speak, so we have to look for these clinical signs…but we still use the term *symptoms* in the book.

Medicine is a constantly changing art, of course with scientific input as well. Things alter as we learn more and more about basic sciences such as genetics and biochemistry and have use of more sophisticated imaging techniques like Computer Aided Tomography (CAT scans) or Magnetic Resonance Imaging (MRI scans). There is academic dispute about many canine maladies, so different vets treat them in different ways. For example, some vets place a greater emphasis on surgical treatment than others.

SELECTING A VET

Your selection of a vet should be based on personal recommendation for his skills with dogs, and, if possible, especially the Bracco or similar breeds. If the vet is based nearby, it will be helpful because you might have an emergency or need to make multiple visits for treatments.

All vets are licensed and should be capable of dealing with routine medical issues such as infections, injuries, the promotion of health (for example, by vaccination and routine check-ups) and routine surgeries such as neutering/spaying, stitching up wounds and the like. If the problem affecting your dog is more complex, your vet will refer your pet to someone with a more detailed knowledge of what is wrong. This will usually be a specialist who concentrates in the field relevant to your dog's problem (e.g., veterinary dermatology,

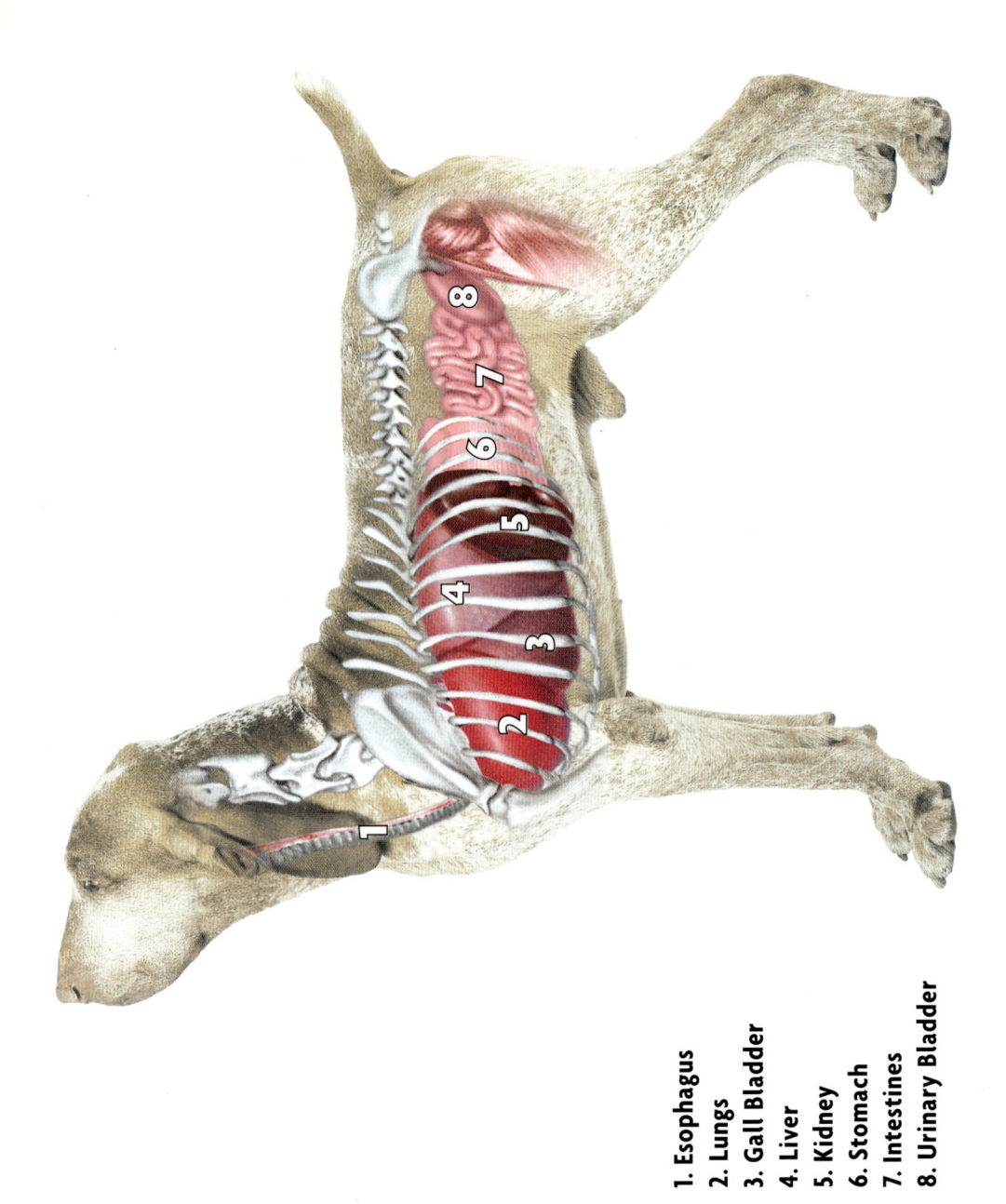

1. Esophagus
2. Lungs
3. Gall Bladder
4. Liver
5. Kidney
6. Stomach
7. Intestines
8. Urinary Bladder

INTERNAL ORGANS OF THE BRACCO ITALIANO

ophthalmology, oncology, etc.).
   Veterinary procedures are very costly and, as the treatments available improve, they are going to become more expensive. It is quite acceptable to get a second opinion, although it is courteous to advise the vets concerned that you are doing so. It is also quite acceptable to discuss matters of cost with your vet; if there is more than one treatment option, cost may be a factor in deciding which route to take.

PREVENTATIVE MEDICINE
It is much easier, less costly and more effective to practice preventative medicine than to fight bouts of illness and disease. Properly bred puppies of all breeds come from parents that were selected based upon their genetic-disease profiles. The puppies' mother should have been vaccinated, free of all internal and external parasites and properly nourished. For these reasons, a visit to the vet who cared for the dam is recommended if at all possible. The dam passes disease resistance to her puppies, which should last from eight to ten weeks. Unfortunately, she can also pass on parasites and infection. This is why knowledge about her health is useful in learning more about the health of the puppies.

WEANING TO FIVE MONTHS OLD
Puppies should be weaned by the time they are two months old. A puppy that remains for at least eight weeks with his mother and littermates usually adapts better to other dogs and people later in life.
   Sometimes new owners have their puppy examined by a vet immediately, which is a good idea unless the puppy is overtired by a long journey. In that case, an appointment should be made for the pup within the next day or so.
   The puppy will have his teeth examined and his skeletal conformation and general health checked prior to certification by the vet. Puppies in certain breeds have problems with their kneecaps, cataracts and other eye problems, heart murmurs and undescended testicles. Your vet might also have training in temperament testing and evaluation. At the first visit, the vet will set up the schedule for your pup's vaccination program.

Breakdown of Veterinary Income by Category

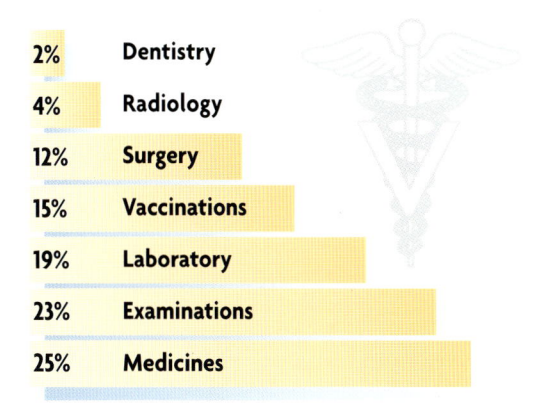

%	Category
2%	Dentistry
4%	Radiology
12%	Surgery
15%	Vaccinations
19%	Laboratory
23%	Examinations
25%	Medicines

A typical vet's income, categorized according to services performed. This survey dealt with small-animal (pets) practices.

SKELETAL STRUCTURE OF THE BRACCO ITALIANO

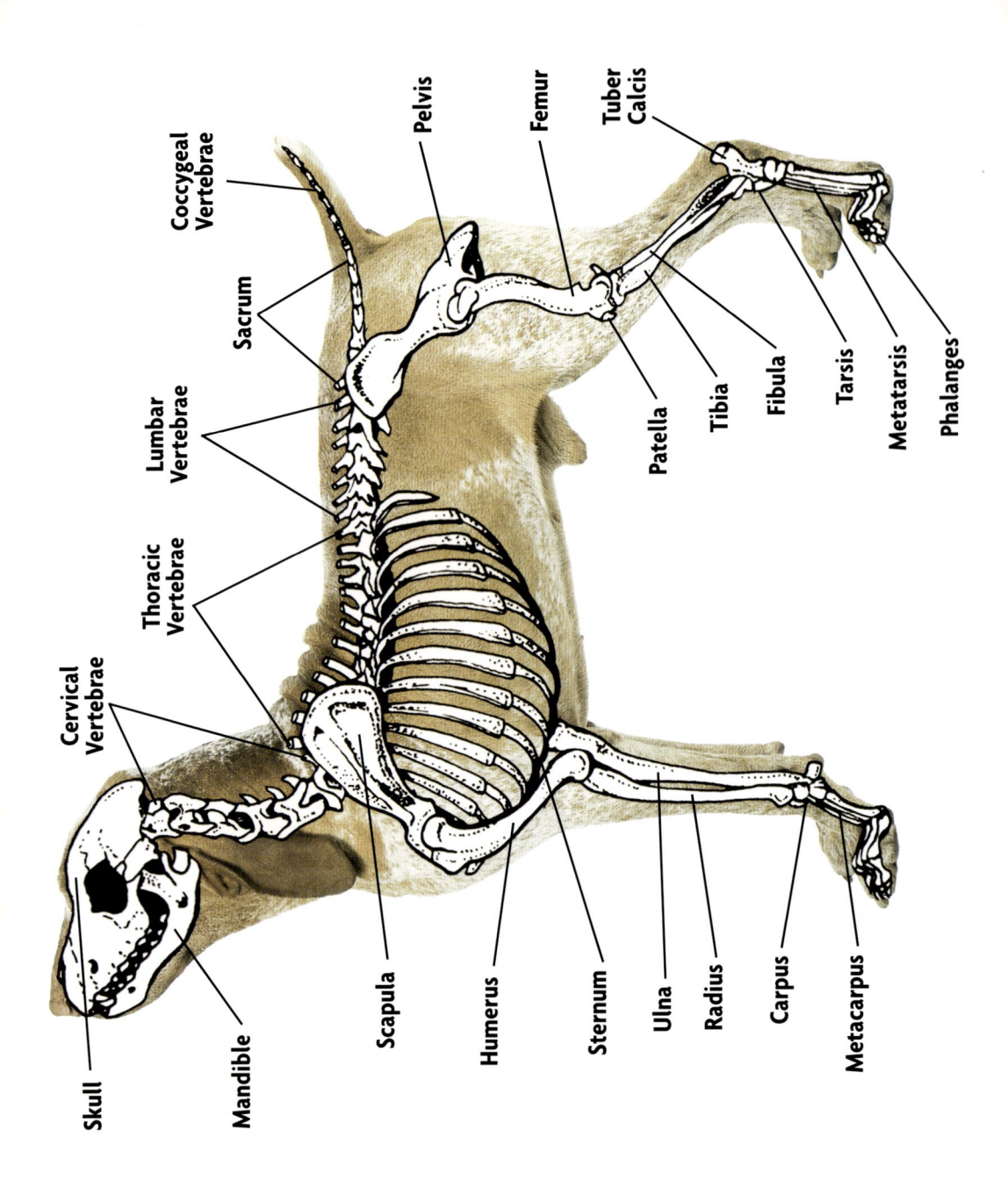

VACCINATIONS

Most vaccinations are given by injection and should only be given by a veterinarian. Both he and you should keep a record of the date of the injection, the identification of the vaccine and the amount given. Some veterinarians give a first vaccination at six weeks, but some dog breeders prefer the course not to commence until about eight weeks because of the risk of interaction with the antibodies produced by the mother. The vaccination schedule is usually based on a two- to four-week cycle. You must take your vet's advice as to when to vaccinate, as this may differ according to the vaccine used.

The usual vaccines contain immunizing doses of several different viruses such as distemper, parvovirus, parainfluenza and hepatitis. There are other vaccines available when the puppy is at risk. You should rely upon professional advice. This is especially true for the booster immunizations. Most vaccination programs require a booster when the puppy is a year old and once a year thereafter. In some cases, circumstances may require more or less frequent immunizations.

HEALTH AND VACCINATION SCHEDULE

AGE IN WEEKS:	6TH	8TH	10TH	12TH	14TH	16TH	20-24TH	52ND
Worm Control	✔	✔	✔	✔	✔	✔	✔	
Neutering							✔	
Heartworm		✔		✔		✔	✔	
Parvovirus	✔		✔		✔		✔	✔
Distemper		✔		✔		✔		✔
Hepatitis		✔		✔		✔		✔
Leptospirosis								✔
Parainfluenza	✔		✔		✔			✔
Dental Examination		✔					✔	✔
Complete Physical		✔					✔	✔
Coronavirus				✔			✔	✔
Canine Cough	✔							
Hip Dysplasia							✔	
Rabies							✔	

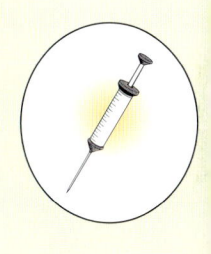

Vaccinations are not instantly effective. It takes about two weeks for the dog's immune system to develop antibodies. Most vaccinations require annual booster shots. Your vet should guide you in this regard.

Canine cough, more formally known as tracheobronchitis, is immunized against with a vaccine that is sprayed into the dog's nostrils. Canine cough is usually included in routine vaccination, but it is often not as effective as the vaccines for other major diseases.

Five Months to One Year of Age

Unless you intend to breed or show your dog, neutering the puppy around six months of age is recommended. Discuss this with your vet; most professionals advise neutering males and spaying females. Neutering/spaying has proven to be extremely beneficial to male and female dogs. Besides eliminating the possibility of pregnancy and pyometra in bitches and testicular cancer in males, it greatly reduces the risk of (but does not prevent) breast cancer in bitches and prostate cancer in males.

Your vet should provide your puppy with a thorough dental evaluation at six months of age, ascertaining whether all of the permanent teeth have erupted

Normal hairs of a dog enlarged 200 times original size. The cuticle (outer covering) is clean and healthy. Unlike human hair that grows from the base, a dog's hair also grows from the end. Damaged hairs and split ends, illustrated above.

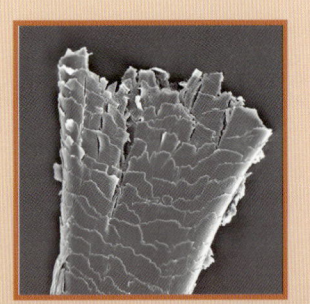

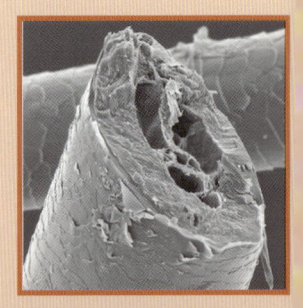

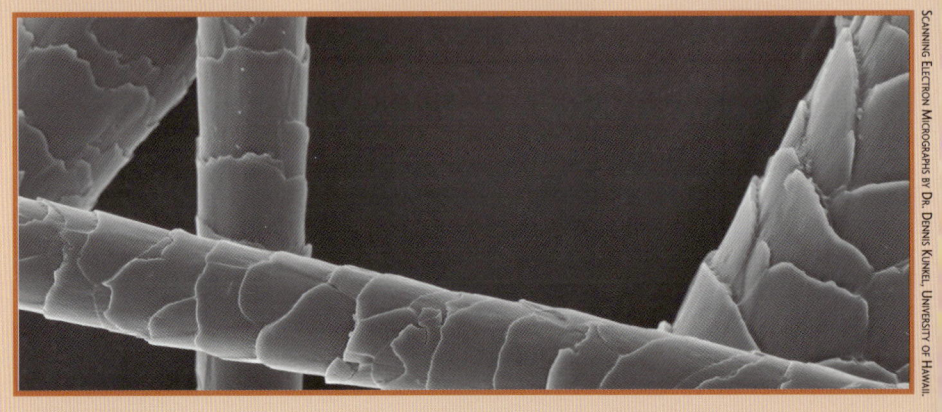

Scanning Electron Micrographs by Dr. Dennis Kunkel, University of Hawaii.

Health Care

DISEASE REFERENCE CHART

	What is it?	What causes it?	Symptoms
Leptospirosis	Severe disease that affects the internal organs; can be spread to people.	A bacterium, which is often carried by rodents, that enters through mucous membranes and spreads quickly throughout the body.	Range from fever, vomiting and loss of appetite in less severe cases to shock, irreversible kidney damage and possibly death in most severe cases.
Rabies	Potentially deadly virus that infects warm-blooded mammals.	Bite from a carrier of the virus, mainly wild animals.	1st stage: dog exhibits change in behavior, fear. 2nd stage: dog's behavior becomes more aggressive. 3rd stage: loss of coordination, trouble with bodily functions.
Parvovirus	Highly contagious virus, potentially deadly.	Ingestion of the virus, which is usually spread through the feces of infected dogs.	Most common: severe diarrhea. Also vomiting, fatigue, lack of appetite.
Canine cough	Contagious respiratory infection.	Combination of types of bacteria and virus. Most common: *Bordetella bronchiseptica* bacteria and parainfluenza virus.	Chronic cough.
Distemper	Disease primarily affecting respiratory and nervous system.	Virus that is related to the human measles virus.	Mild symptoms such as fever, lack of appetite and mucus secretion progress to evidence of brain damage, "hard pad."
Hepatitis	Virus primarily affecting the liver.	Canine adenovirus type I (CAV-1). Enters system when dog breathes in particles.	Lesser symptoms include listlessness, diarrhea, vomiting. More severe symptoms include "blue-eye" (clumps of virus in eye).
Coronavirus	Virus resulting in digestive problems.	Virus is spread through infected dog's feces.	Stomach upset evidenced by lack of appetite, vomiting, diarrhea.

properly. A home dental-care regimen should be initiated at six months, including brushing weekly and providing good dental devices (such as hard plastic or nylon bones). Regular dental care promotes healthy teeth, fresh breath and a longer life.

DOGS OLDER THAN ONE YEAR
Continue to visit the vet at least once a year. There is no such disease as "old age," but bodily functions do change with age. The eyes and ears are no longer as efficient. Liver, kidney and intestinal functions often decline. Proper dietary changes, recommended by your vet, can make life more pleasant for your aging Bracco and you.

SKIN PROBLEMS
Vets are consulted by dog owners for skin problems more than for any other group of diseases or maladies. A dog's skin is as sensitive, if not more so, than human skin, and both can suffer from almost the same ailments, though

> **VITAL SIGNS**
> A dog's normal temperature is 101.5 degrees Fahrenheit. A range of between 100.0 and 102.5 degrees should be considered normal, as each dog's body sets its own temperature. It will be helpful if you take your dog's temperature when you know he is healthy and record it. Then, when you suspect that he is not feeling well, you will have a normal figure to compare the abnormal temperature against.
>
> The normal pulse rate for a dog is between 100 and 125 beats per minute.

the occurrence of acne in most breeds is rare. For this reason, veterinary dermatology has developed into a specialty practiced by many vets.

Although there may be some hereditary element involved in dogs suffering from skin allergies, feeding and environment also play an instrumental role. Common house dust mites, pollen, flea bites and molds are just a few of many things that can have an effect on your Bracco's skin. The ways in which dogs are affected can vary considerably, from a slight reddening of the skin to permanent open sores, coupled with hair loss. Often allergies are more apparent during spring and summer. Dealing with skin allergies is difficult, but it is sensible to seek early veterinary advice as to what remedy is likely to be the most suitable, according to the condition.

Since many skin problems have visual symptoms that are almost identical, it requires the skill of an experienced veterinary dermatologist to identify and cure many of the more severe skin disorders. Pet shops sell many treatments for skin problems, but most of the treatments are directed at symptoms and not at the underlying problem(s). If your dog is suffering from a skin disorder, you should seek professional assistance as quickly as possible. As with all diseases, the earlier a problem is identified and treated, the more likely it is that the cure will be successful.

HEREDITARY SKIN DISORDERS
Veterinary dermatologists are currently researching a number of skin disorders that are believed to have hereditary bases. These inherited diseases are transmitted by both parents, who appear (phenotypically) normal but have a recessive gene for the disease, meaning that they carry, but are not affected by, the disease. These diseases pose serious problems to breeders because in some instances there are no methods of identifying carriers. Often the secondary diseases associated with these skin conditions are even more debilitating than the skin disorders themselves, including cancers and respiratory problems.

First Aid at a Glance

Burns
Place the affected area under cool water; use ice if only a small area is burnt.

Bee stings/Insect bites
Apply ice to relieve swelling; antihistamine dosed properly.

Animal bites
Clean any bleeding area; apply pressure until bleeding subsides; go to the vet.

Spider bites
Use cold compress and a pressurized pack to inhibit venom's spreading.

Antifreeze poisoning
Induce vomiting with hydrogen peroxide. Seek *immediate* veterinary help!

Fish hooks
Removal best handled by vet; hook must be cut in order to remove.

Snake bites
Pack ice around bite; contact vet quickly; identify snake for proper antivenin.

Car accident
Move dog from roadway with blanket; seek veterinary aid.

Shock
Calm the dog; keep him warm; seek immediate veterinary help.

Nosebleed
Apply cold compress to the nose; apply pressure to any visible abrasion.

Bleeding
Apply pressure above the area; treat wound by applying a cotton pack.

Heat stroke
Submerge dog in cold bath; cool down with fresh air and water; go to the vet.

Frostbite/Hypothermia
Warm the dog with a warm bath, electric blankets or hot water bottles.

Abrasions
Clean the wound and wash out thoroughly with fresh water; apply antiseptic.

!! *Remember: an injured dog may attempt to bite a helping hand from fear and confusion. Always muzzle the dog before trying to offer assistance.* !!

Among the hereditary skin disorders, for which the mode of inheritance is known, are acrodermatitis, cutaneous asthenia (Ehlers-Danlos syndrome), sebaceous adenitis, cyclic hematopoiesis, dermatomyositis, IgA deficiency, color dilution alopecia and nodular dermatofibrosis. Some of these disorders are limited to one or two breeds, while others affect a large number of breeds. All inherited diseases must be diagnosed and treated by a veterinary specialist.

PARASITE BITES
Many of us are allergic to insect bites. The bites itch, erupt and may even become infected. Dogs have the same reaction to fleas, ticks and/or mites. When an insect lands on you, you have the chance to whisk it away with your hand. Unfortunately, when a dog is bitten by a flea, tick or mite, he can only scratch it away or bite it. By the time the dog has been bitten, the parasite has done some of its damage. It may also have laid eggs, which will cause further problems in the near future. The itching from parasite bites is probably due to the saliva injected into the site when the parasite sucks the dog's blood.

AIRBORNE ALLERGIES
Just as humans suffer from hay fever during the pollinating season, many dogs suffer from the same allergies. When the pollen count is high, your dog might suffer, but don't expect him to sneeze and have a runny nose as a human would. Dogs react to pollen allergies in the same way they react to fleas—they scratch and bite themselves. Dogs, like humans, can be tested for allergens. Discuss the testing with your vet.

ACRAL LICK GRANULOMA
Many large dogs have a very poorly understood syndrome called acral lick granuloma. The manifestation of the problem is the dog's tireless attack at a specific area of the body, almost always the legs or paws. The dog licks so intensively that he removes the hair and skin, leaving an ugly, large wound. Tiny protuberances, which are outgrowths of new capillaries, bead on the surface of the wound. Owners who notice their dogs' biting and chewing at their extremities should have the vet determine the cause. If lick granuloma is identified, although there is no absolute cure, corticosteroids are the most common treatment.

AUTO-IMMUNE ILLNESSES
An auto-immune illness is one in which the immune system overacts and does not recognize parts of the affected person (or dog); rather, the immune system starts to react as if these parts were foreign and need to be destroyed. An example is

rheumatoid arthritis, which occurs when the body does not recognize the joints, thus leading to a very painful and damaging reaction in the joints. This has nothing to do with age, so can occur in children and young dogs. The wear-and-tear arthritis of the older person or dog is osteoarthritis.

Lupus is an auto-immune disease that affects dogs as well as people. It can take variable forms, affecting the kidneys, bones and skin. It can be fatal, so is treated with steroids, which can themselves have very significant side effects. The steroids calm down the allergic reaction to the body's tissues, which helps the lupus, but steroids also calm down the body's reaction to real foreign substances such as bacteria, and also thin the skin and bone.

FOOD PROBLEMS

FOOD ALLERGIES

Some dogs can be allergic to many foods that may be best-sellers and highly recommended by breeders and vets. Changing the brand of food that you buy may not eliminate the problem if the element to which the dog is allergic is contained in the new brand.

Recognizing a food allergy in a dog can be difficult. Humans often have rashes when they eat foods to which they are allergic, or have swelling of the lips or eyes. Dogs do not usually develop rashes, but react in the same way as they do to an airborne or bite allergy—they itch, scratch and bite. While pollen allergies are usually seasonal, food allergies are year-round problems.

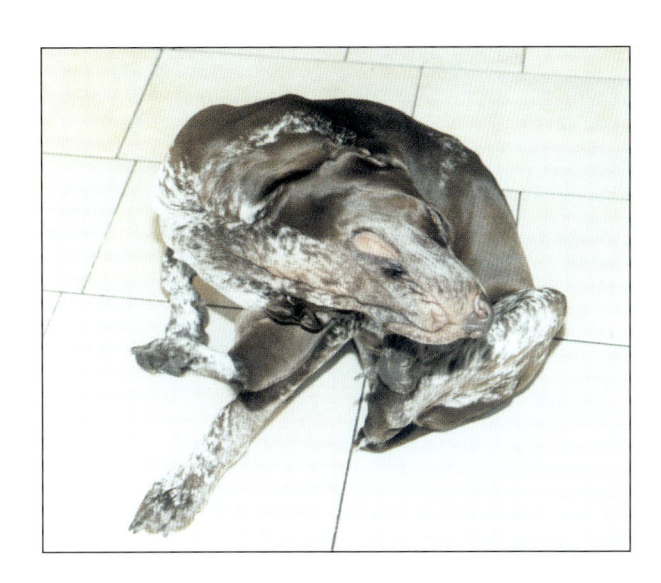

TREATING FOOD ALLERGY

Diagnosis of food allergy is based on a two- to four-week dietary trial with a home-cooked diet fed to the exclusion of all other foods. The diet should consist of boiled rice or potato with a source of protein that the dog has never eaten before. Ingredients like chopped beef and chicken are common in dogs' diets, so try another protein source such as fresh or frozen fish, lamb or even something as exotic as pheasant. Water has to be the only drink, and it is really important that no other foods are fed during this trial. If the dog's condition improves, you will need to try the

What's itching your Bracco? All dogs need a good scratch now and then, but be vigilant in checking your dog's skin and coat to make sure he's not suffering from allergies, parasites or problems from other irritants.

original diet once again to see if the itching resumes. If it does, then this confirms the diagnosis that the dog is allergic to his original diet. The treatment is long-term feeding of something that does not distress the dog's skin, which may be in the form of one of the commercially available hypoallergenic diets or the home-made diet that you created for the allergy trial.

Food Intolerance

Food intolerance is the inability of the dog to completely digest certain foods. This occurs because the dog does not have the chemicals necessary to digest some foodstuffs. These chemicals are called enzymes. For example, all puppies have the enzymes necessary to digest canine milk, but some dogs do not have the enzymes to digest a very different form of milk that is commonly found in human households—milk from cows. In such dogs, drinking cows' milk results in loose bowels, stomach pains and the passage of gas.

> **VACCINE ALLERGIES**
> Vaccines do not work all the time. Sometimes dogs are allergic to them and many times the antibodies, which are supposed to be stimulated by the vaccine, just are not produced. You should keep your dog in the veterinary clinic for an hour after he is vaccinated to be sure there are no allergic reactions.

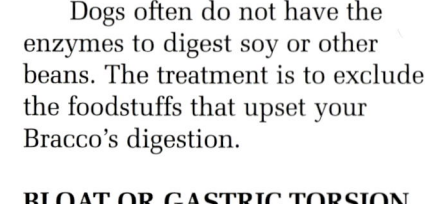

Dogs often do not have the enzymes to digest soy or other beans. The treatment is to exclude the foodstuffs that upset your Bracco's digestion.

BLOAT OR GASTRIC TORSION

This is the greatest killer of the large, deep-chested breeds, and is the subject of much research, but still manages to take away many dogs before their time and in a very horrible way. A cross-section through a Bracco would show how deep the body cavity is. There are muscles around the vertebrae that give strength to the back and allow it to be flexed and stretched when running. The stomach hangs like a handbag with both straps broken within this deep body cavity.

There is another way in which the stomach is held in place. There is support provided by the junction with the esophagus or gullet, and there is support provided by the junction with the first part of the small intestine, the "broken straps of the handbag." The only other support is a thin layer of partially opaque "internal skin" called the peritoneum.

It is no wonder that the stomach can move around easily. Those breeds with the deepest chests are at the greatest risk of having their whole stomachs twist around (gastric torsion). This cuts off the blood supply and prevents the stomach's contents from leaving, and increases the amount of gas in

Health Care

the stomach. Once these things have happened, surgery is vital. If the blood supply has been cut off too long and a bit of the stomach wall dies, death of the dog is almost inevitable.

The horrendous pain of this condition is due to the stomach wall's being stretched by the gas caught in the stomach, as well as the stomach wall's desperately needing the blood that cannot get to it. There is the pain of not being able to pass a much greater than normal amount of wind; added to this is a pain equivalent to that of a heart attack, which is due to the heart muscle's being starved of blood.

TRY TO PREVENT BLOAT

Here are some tips on how to reduce the risk of bloat in your Bracco Italiano:
- Do not exercise your Bracco immediately before or after feeding; let at least an hour elapse between the two;
- Do not feed cheap food with high cereal content;
- Feed high-quality, low-residue diets;
- Elevate food and water bowls to try to reduce any air swallowed;
- If your Bracco is greedy and eats quickly, reduce the air swallowed by putting something large and inedible in the food bowl so that the dog has to pick around the object and thus eat more slowly;
- Limit water intake at mealtimes and never let your Bracco gulp water.

DETECTING BLOAT

The following are symptoms of bloat and require immediate veterinary attention:
- Your dog's stomach starts to distend, ending up large and as tight as a basketball;
- Your dog is dribbling, as no saliva can be swallowed;
- Your dog makes frequent attempts to vomit but cannot bring anything up due to the stomach's being closed off;
- Your dog is distressed from pain;
- Your dog starts to suffer from clinical shock, meaning that there is not enough blood in the dog's circulation as the hard, dilated stomach stops the blood from returning to the heart to be pumped around the body. Clinical shock is indicated by pale gums and tongue, as they have been starved of blood. The shocked dog also has glazed, staring eyes.

You have minutes—yes *minutes*—to get your dog into surgery. If you see any of these symptoms at any time of the day or night, get to the vet immediately. Someone will have to phone and advise that you are on your way (which is a justification for the invention of the cellular phone!) so that they can be prepared to get your pet on the operating table.

A male dog flea, *Ctenocephalides canis*.

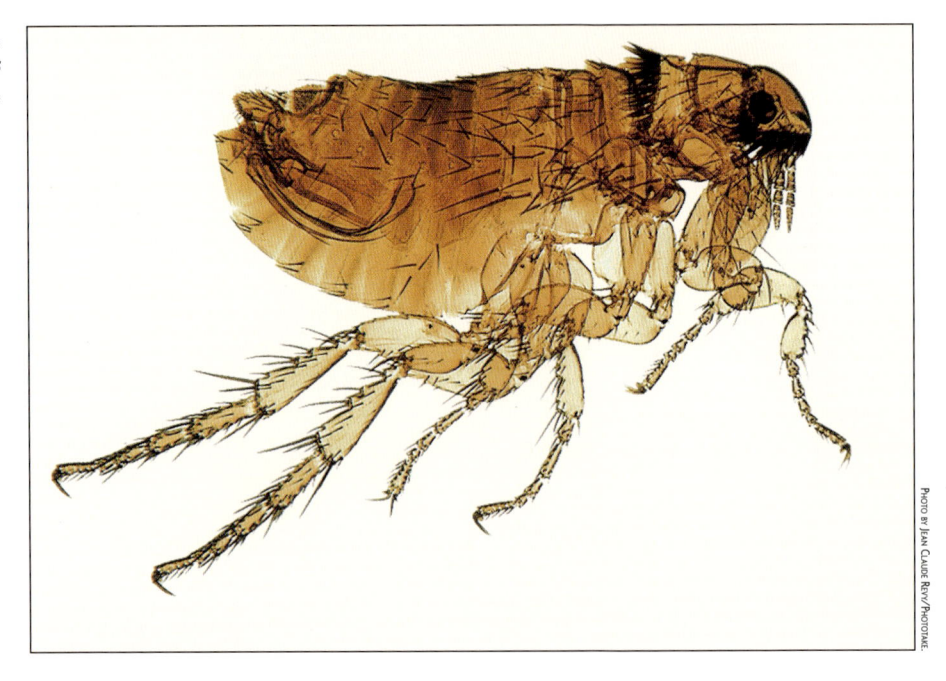

EXTERNAL PARASITES

Fleas

Of all the problems to which dogs are prone, none is more well known and frustrating than fleas. Flea infestation is relatively simple to cure but difficult to prevent. Parasites that are harbored inside the body are a bit more difficult to eradicate but they are easier to control.

To control flea infestation, you have to understand the flea's life cycle. Fleas are often thought of as a summertime problem, but centrally heated homes have changed the patterns and fleas can be found at any time of the year. The most effective method of flea control is a two-stage approach: one stage to kill the adult fleas, and the other to control the development of pre-adult fleas. Unfortunately, no single active ingredient is effective against all stages of the life cycle.

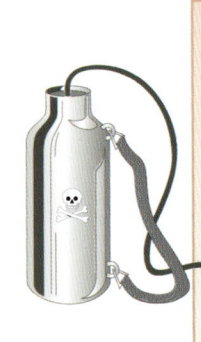

> **FLEA KILLER CAUTION—"POISON"**
>
> Flea-killers are poisonous. You should not spray these toxic chemicals on areas of a dog's body that he licks, including his genitals and his face. Flea killers taken internally are a better answer, but check with your vet in case internal therapy is not advised for your dog.

Health Care

LIFE CYCLE STAGES
During its life, a flea will pass through four life stages: egg, larva, pupa or nymph and adult. The adult stage is the most visible and irritating stage of the flea life cycle, and this is why the majority of flea-control products concentrate on this stage. The fact is that adult fleas account for only 1% of the total flea population, and the other 99% exist in pre-adult stages, i.e., eggs, larvae and nymphs. The pre-adult stages are barely visible to the naked eye.

THE LIFE CYCLE OF THE FLEA
Eggs are laid on the dog, usually in quantities of about 20 or 30, several times a day. The adult female flea must have a blood meal before each egg-laying session. When first laid, the eggs will cling to the dog's hair, as the eggs are still moist. However, they will quickly dry out and fall from the dog, especially if the dog moves around or scratches. Many eggs will fall off in the dog's favorite area or an area in which he spends a lot of time, such as his bed.

Once the eggs fall from the dog onto the carpet or furniture, they will hatch into larvae. This takes from one to ten days. Larvae are not particularly mobile and will usually travel only a few inches from where they hatch. However, they do have a tendency to move away from bright light and heavy traffic—under furniture and behind doors are common places to find high quantities of flea larvae.

The flea larvae feed on dead organic matter, including adult flea feces, until they are ready to change into adult fleas. Fleas will usually remain as larvae for around seven days. After this period, the larvae will pupate into protective pupae. While inside the pupae, the larvae will undergo metamorphosis and change into

> **EN GARDE:**
> **CATCHING FLEAS OFF GUARD!**
> Consider the following ways to arm yourself against fleas:
> - Add a small amount of pennyroyal or eucalyptus oil to your dog's bath. These natural remedies repel fleas.
> - Supplement your dog's food with fresh garlic (minced or grated) and a hearty amount of brewer's yeast, both of which ward off fleas.
> - Use a flea comb on your dog daily. Submerge fleas in a cup of bleach to kill them quickly.
> - Confine the dog to only a few rooms to limit the spread of fleas in the home.
> - Vacuum daily...and get all of the crevices! Dispose of the bag every few days until the problem is under control.
> - Wash your dog's bedding daily. Cover cushions where your dog sleeps with towels, and wash the towels often.

Fleas have been measured as being able to jump 300,000 times and can jump over 150 times their length in any direction, including straight up.

adult fleas. This can take as little time as a few days, but the adult fleas can remain inside the pupae waiting to hatch for up to two years. The pupae are signaled to hatch by certain stimuli, such as physical pressure—the pupae's being stepped on, heat from an animal's lying on the pupae or increased carbon-dioxide levels and vibrations—indicating that a suitable host is available.

Once hatched, the adult flea must feed within a few days. Once the adult flea finds a host, it will not leave voluntarily. It only becomes dislodged by grooming or the host animal's scratching. The adult flea will remain on the host for the duration of its life unless forcibly removed.

Treating the Environment and the Dog

Treating fleas should be a two-pronged attack. First, the environment needs to be treated; this includes carpets and furniture, especially the dog's bedding and areas underneath furniture. The environment should be treated with a household spray containing an Insect Growth Regulator (IGR) and an insecticide to kill the adult fleas. Most IGRs are effective against eggs and larvae; they actually mimic the fleas' own hormones and stop the eggs and larvae from developing into adult fleas. There are currently no treatments available to attack the pupa stage of the life cycle, so the adult insecticide is used to kill the newly hatched adult fleas before they find a host. Most IGRs are active for many months, while adult insecticides are only active for a few days.

A scanning electron micrograph of a dog or cat flea, *Ctenocephalides*, magnified more than 100x. This image has been colorized for effect.

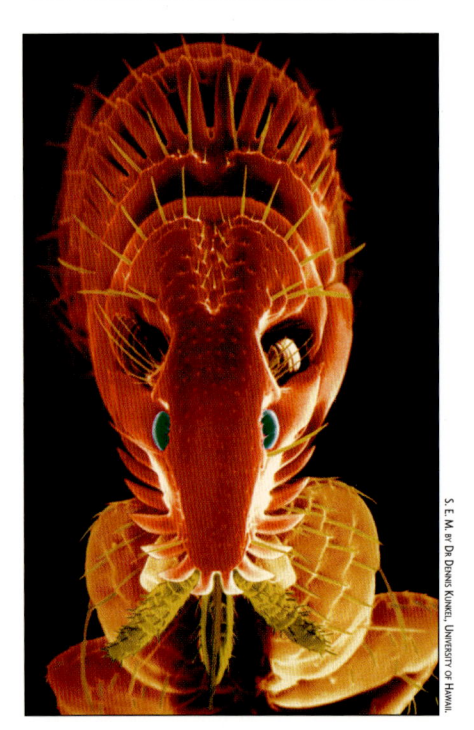

THE LIFE CYCLE OF THE FLEA

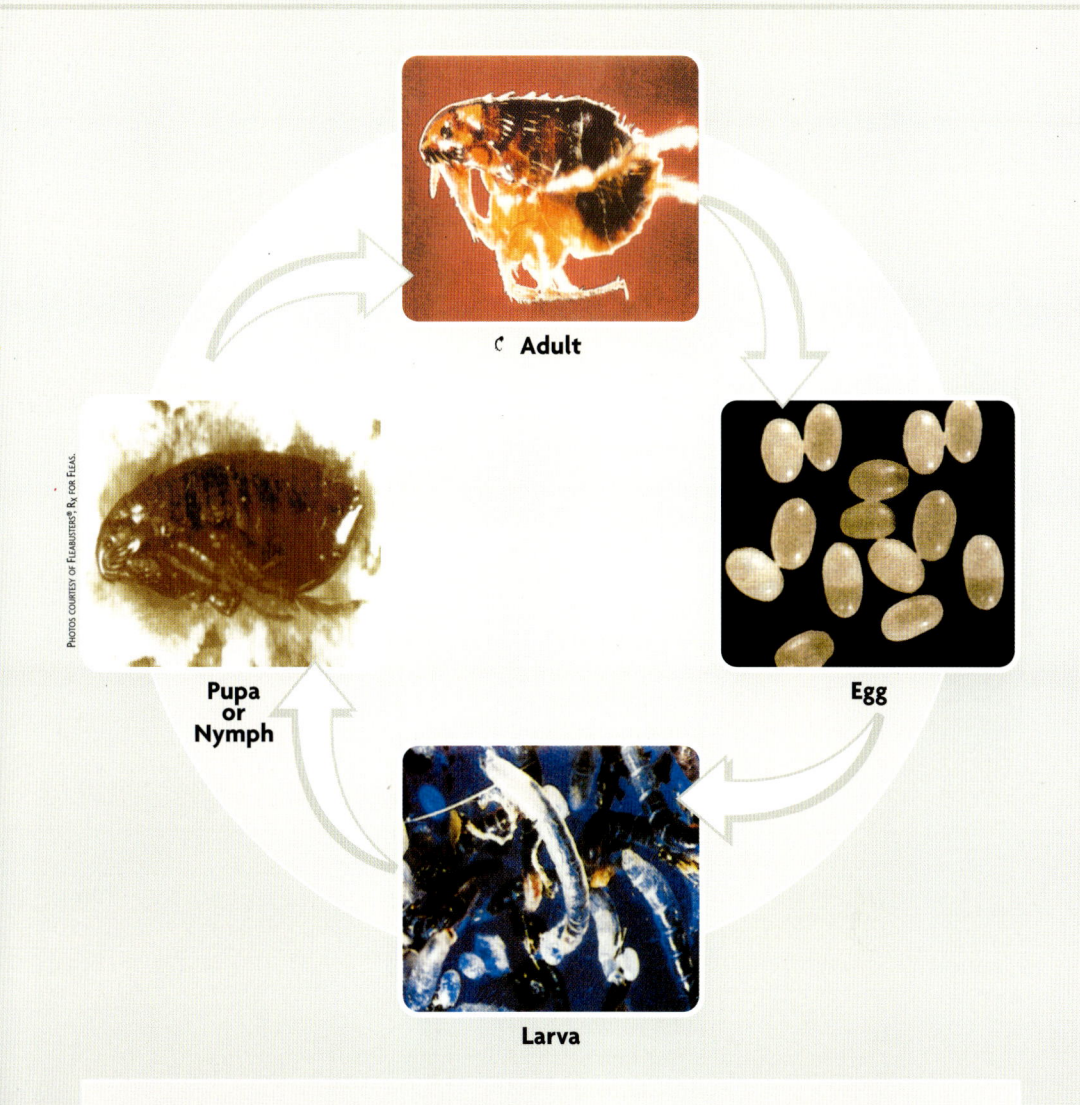

Adult

Egg

Larva

Pupa or Nymph

Fleas have been around for millions of years and have adapted to changing host animals. They are able to go through a complete life cycle in less than one month or they can extend their lives to almost two years by remaining as pupae or cocoons. They do not need blood or any other food for up to 20 months.

INSECT GROWTH REGULATOR (IGR)

Two types of products should be used when treating fleas—a product to treat the pet and a product to treat the home. Adult fleas represent less than 1% of the flea population. The pre-adult fleas (eggs, larvae and pupae) represent more than 99% of the flea population and are found in the environment; it is in the case of pre-adult fleas that products containing an Insect Growth Regulator (IGR) should be used in the home.

IGRs are a new class of compounds used to prevent the development of insects. They do not kill the insect outright, but instead use the insect's biology against it to stop it from completing its growth. Products that contain methoprene are the world's first and leading IGRs. Used to control fleas and other insects, this type of IGR will stop flea larvae from developing and protect the house for up to seven months.

The American dog tick, *Dermacentor variabilis*, is probably the most common tick found on dogs. Look at the strength in its eight legs! No wonder it's hard to detach them.

When treating with a household spray, it is a good idea to vacuum before applying the product. This stimulates as many pupae as possible to hatch into adult fleas. The vacuum cleaner should also be treated with an insecticide to prevent the eggs and larvae that have been collected in the vacuum bag from hatching.

The second stage of treatment is to apply an adult insecticide to the dog. Traditionally, this would be in the form of a collar or a spray, but more recent innovations include digestible insecticides that poison the fleas when they ingest the dog's blood. Alternatively, there are drops that, when placed on the back of the dog's neck, spread throughout the hair and skin to kill adult fleas.

TICKS

Though not as common as fleas, ticks are found all over the tropical and temperate world. They don't bite, like fleas; they harpoon. They dig their sharp proboscis (nose) into the dog's skin and drink the blood. Their only food and drink is dog's blood. Dogs can get Lyme

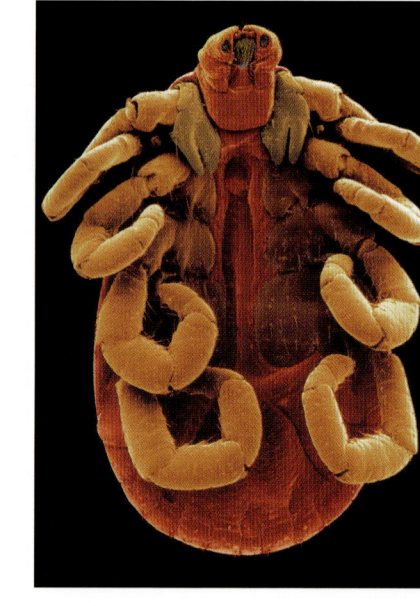

Health Care

disease, Rocky Mountain spotted fever, tick bite paralysis and many other diseases from ticks. They may live where fleas are found and they like to hide in cracks or seams in walls. They are controlled the same way fleas are controlled.

The American dog tick, *Dermacentor variabilis*, may well be the most common dog tick in many geographical areas, especially those areas where the climate is hot and humid. Most dog ticks have life expectancies of a week to six months, depending upon climatic conditions. They can neither jump nor fly, but they can crawl slowly and can range up to 16 feet to reach a sleeping or unsuspecting dog.

MITES

Just as fleas and ticks can be problematic for your dog, mites can also lead to an itchy nuisance. Microscopic in size, mites are related to ticks and generally take up permanent residence on their host animal—in this case, your dog! The term *mange* refers to any infestation caused by one of the mighty mites, of which there are six varieties that concern dog owners.

Demodex mites cause a condition known as demodicosis (sometimes called red mange or follicular mange), in which the mites live in the dog's hair follicles and sebaceous glands in

DEER-TICK CROSSING

The great outdoors may be fun for your dog, but it also is a home to dangerous ticks. Deer ticks carry a bacterium known as *Borrelia burgdorferi* and are most active in the autumn and spring. When infections are caught early, penicillin and tetracycline are effective antibiotics, but, if left untreated, the bacteria may cause neurological, kidney and cardiac problems as well as long-term trouble with walking and painful joints.

The head of an American dog tick, *Dermacentor variabilis*, enlarged and colorized for effect.

The mange mite, *Psoroptes bovis*, can infest cattle and other domestic animals.

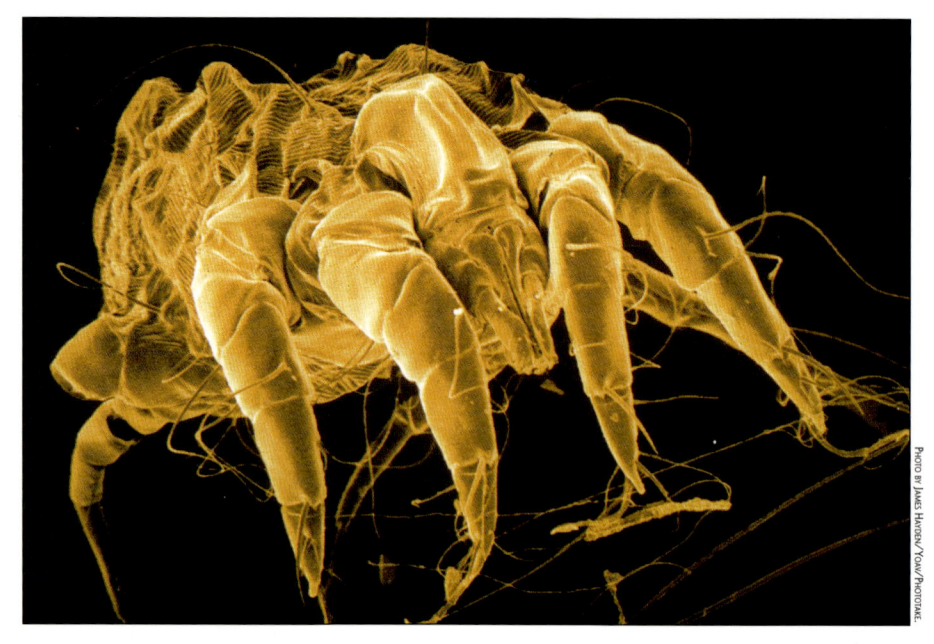

Human lice look like dog lice; the two are closely related.
Photo by Dwight R. Kuhn.

larger-than-normal numbers. This type of mange is commonly passed from the dam to her puppies and usually shows up on the puppies' muzzles, though demodicosis is not transferable from one normal dog to another. Most dogs recover from this type of mange without any treatment, though topical therapies are commonly prescribed by the vet.

The *Cheyletiellosis* mite is the hook-mouthed culprit associated with "walking dandruff," a condition that affects dogs as well as cats and rabbits. This mite lives on the surface of the animal's skin and is readily transferable through direct or indirect contact with an affected animal. The dandruff is present in the form of scaly skin, which may or may not be itchy. If not treated, this mange can affect a whole kennel of dogs and can be spread to humans as well.

The *Sarcoptes* mite causes intense itching on the dog in the form of a condition known as scabies or sarcoptic mange. The cycle of the *Sarcoptes* mite lasts about three weeks, and the mites live in the top layer of the dog's skin (epidermis), preferably in areas with little hair. Scabies is highly contagious and can be passed to humans. Sometimes an allergic reaction to the mite worsens the severe itching associated with sarcoptic mange.

Ear mites, *Otodectes cynotis*, lead to otodectic mange, which most commonly affects the outer ear canal of the dog, though other areas can be affected as well. Dogs with ear-mite infestation commonly scratch at their ears, causing further irritation, and shake their heads. Dark brown droppings in the outer ear confirm the diagnosis. Your vet can prescribe a treatment to flush out the ears and kill any eggs in the ears. A complete month of treatment is necessary to cure the mange.

Two other mites, less common in dogs, include *Dermanyssus gallinae* (the poultry or red mite) and *Eutrombicula alfreddugesi* (the North American mite associated with trombiculidiasis or chigger infestation). The poultry mite frequently lives on chickens, but can transfer to dogs who spend time near farm animals. Chigger infestation affects dogs in the Central US who have exposure to woodlands. The types of mange caused by both of these mites are treatable by vets.

> **NOT A DROP TO DRINK**
> Never allow your dog to swim in polluted water or public areas where water quality can be suspect. Even perfectly clear water can harbor parasites, many of which can cause serious to fatal illnesses in canines. Areas inhabited by waterfowl and other wildlife are especially dangerous.

> **DO NOT MIX**
> Never mix parasite-control products without first consulting your vet. Some products can become toxic when combined with others and can cause fatal consequences.

INTERNAL PARASITES

Most animals—fishes, birds and mammals, including dogs and humans—have worms and other parasites that live inside their bodies. According to Dr. Herbert R. Axelrod, the fish pathologist, there are two kinds of parasites: dumb and smart. The smart parasites live in peaceful cooperation with their hosts (symbiosis), while the dumb parasites kill their hosts. Most worm infections are relatively easy to control. If they are not controlled, they weaken the host dog to the point that other medical problems occur, but they do not kill the host as dumb parasites would.

A brown dog tick, *Rhipicephalus sanguineus*, is an uncommon but annoying tick found on dogs.
PHOTO BY CAROLINA BIOLOGICAL SUPPLY/PHOTOTAKE.

BRACCO ITALIANO

The roundworm Rhabditis can infect both dogs and humans.

The roundworm, Ascaris lumbricoides.

ROUNDWORMS

Average-size dogs can pass 1,360,000 roundworm eggs every day. For example, if there were only 1 million dogs in the world, the world would be saturated with thousands of tons of dog feces. These feces would contain around 15,000,000,000 roundworm eggs.

Up to 31% of home yards and children's sand boxes in the US contain roundworm eggs.

Flushing dog's feces down the toilet is not a safe practice because the usual sewage treatments do not destroy roundworm eggs.

Infected puppies start shedding roundworm eggs at three weeks of age. They can be infected by their mother's milk.

ROUNDWORMS

The roundworms that infect dogs are known scientifically as *Toxocara canis*. They live in the dog's intestines and shed eggs continually. It has been estimated that a dog produces about 6 or more ounces of feces every day. Each ounce of feces averages hundreds of thousands of roundworm eggs. There are no known areas in which dogs roam that do not contain roundworm eggs. The greatest danger of roundworms is that they infect people, too! It is wise to have your dog tested regularly for roundworms.

In young puppies, roundworms cause bloated bellies, diarrhea, coughing and vomiting, and are transmitted from the dam (through blood or milk). Affected puppies will not appear as animated as normal puppies. The worms appear spaghetti-like, measuring as long as 6 inches. Adult dogs can acquire roundworms through coprophagia (eating contaminated feces) or by killing rodents that carry roundworms.

Roundworm infection can kill puppies and cause severe problems in adults, as the hatched larvae travel to the lungs and trachea through the bloodstream. Cleanliness is the best preventative for roundworms. Always pick up after your dog and dispose of feces in appropriate receptacles.

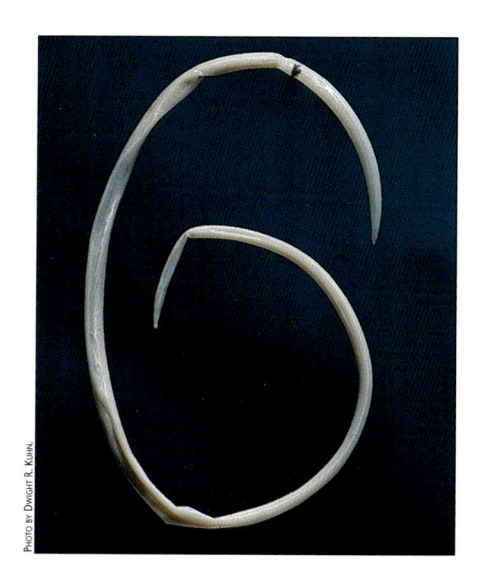

The hookworm, Ancylostoma caninum.

HOOKWORMS

In the United States, dog owners have to be concerned about four different species of hookworm, the most common and most serious of which is *Ancylostoma caninum,* which prefers warm climates. The others are *Ancylostoma braziliense, Ancylostoma tubaeforme* and *Uncinaria stenocephala,* the latter of which is a concern to dogs living in the northern US and Canada, as this species prefers cold climates. Hookworms are dangerous to humans as well as to dogs and cats, and can be the cause of severe anemia due to iron deficiency. The worm uses its teeth to attach itself to the dog's intestines and changes the site of its attachment about six times per day. Each time the worm repositions itself, the dog loses blood and can become anemic. *Ancylostoma caninum* is the most likely of the four species to cause anemia in the dog.

Symptoms of hookworm infection include dark stools, weight loss, general weakness, pale coloration and anemia, as well as possible skin problems. Fortunately, hookworms are easily purged from the affected dog with a number of medications that have proven effective. Discuss these with your vet. Most heartworm preventatives include a hookworm insecticide as well.

Owners also must be aware that hookworms can infect humans, who can acquire the larvae through exposure to contaminated feces. Since the worms cannot complete their life cycle on a human, the worms simply infest the skin and cause irritation. This condition is known as cutaneous larva migrans syndrome. As a preventative, use disposable gloves or a "poop-scoop" to pick up your dog's droppings and prevent your dog (or neighborhood cats) from defecating in children's play areas.

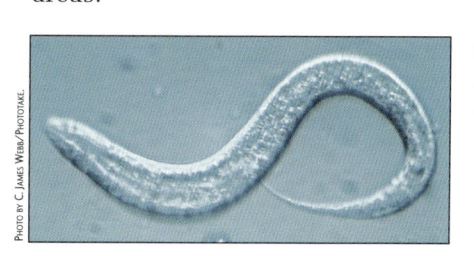

The infective stage of the hookworm larva.

TAPEWORMS

Humans, rats, squirrels, foxes, coyotes, wolves and domestic dogs are all susceptible to tapeworm infection. Except in humans, tapeworms are usually not a fatal infection. Infected individuals can harbor 1000 parasitic worms.

Tapeworms, like some other types of worm, are hermaphroditic, meaning male and female in the same worm.

If dogs eat infected rats or mice, or anything else infected with tapeworm, they get the tapeworm disease. One month after attaching to a dog's intestine, the worm starts shedding eggs. These eggs are infective immediately. Infective eggs can live for a few months without a host animal.

The head and rostellum (the round prominence on the scolex) of a tapeworm, which infects dogs and humans.

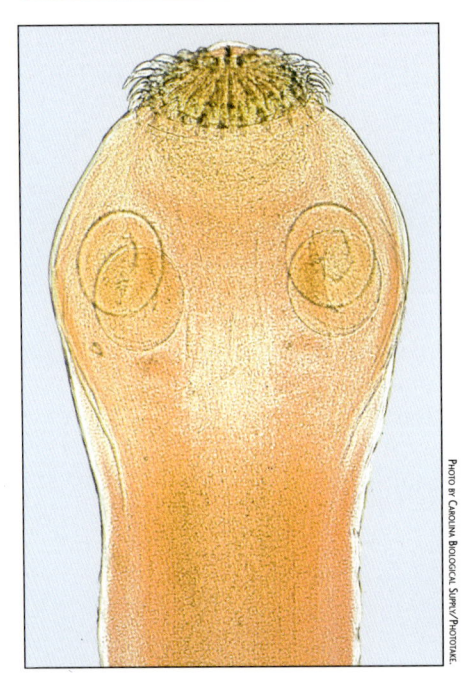

TAPEWORMS

There are many species of tapeworm, all of which are carried by fleas! The most common tapeworm affecting dogs is known as *Dipylidium caninum*. The dog eats the flea and starts the tapeworm cycle. Humans can also be infected with tapeworms—so don't eat fleas! Fleas are so small that your dog could pass them onto your hands, your plate or your food and thus make it possible for you to ingest a flea that is carrying tapeworm eggs.

While tapeworm infection is not life-threatening in dogs (smart parasite!), it can be the cause of a very serious liver disease for humans. About 50% of the humans infected with *Echinococcus multilocularis*, a type of tapeworm that causes alveolar hydatid, perish.

WHIPWORMS

In North America, whipworms are counted among the most common parasitic worms in dogs. The whipworm's scientific name is *Trichuris vulpis*. These worms attach themselves in the lower parts of the intestine, where they feed. Affected dogs may only experience upset tummies, colic and diarrhea. These worms, however, can live for months or years in the dog, beginning their larval stage in the small intestine, spending their adult stage in the large intestine and finally passing infective eggs through the dog's feces. The only way to detect whipworms is through a fecal examination, though this is not always foolproof. Treatment for whipworms is tricky, due to the worms' unusual life-cycle pattern, and very often dogs are reinfected due to exposure to infective eggs on the ground. The whipworm eggs can survive in the environment for as long as five years; thus, cleaning up droppings in your own backyard as well as in public places is absolutely essential for sanitation purposes and the health of your dog and others.

THREADWORMS

Though less common than roundworms, hookworms and those previously mentioned, threadworms concern dog owners in the southwestern US and Gulf Coast area where the climate is hot and humid. Living in the small intestine of the dog, this worm measures a mere 2 millimeters and is round in shape. Like that of the whipworm, the threadworm's life cycle is very complex and the eggs and larvae are passed through the feces. A deadly disease in humans, *Strongyloides* readily infects people, and the handling of feces is the most common means of transmission. Threadworms are most often seen in young puppies; bloody diarrhea and pneumonia are symptoms. Sick puppies must be isolated and treated immediately; vets recommend a follow-up treatment one month later.

HEARTWORM PREVENTATIVES

There are many heartworm preventatives on the market, many of which are sold at your veterinarian's office. These products can be given daily or monthly, depending on the manufacturer's instructions. All of these preventatives contain chemical insecticides directed at killing heartworms, which leads to some controversy among dog owners. In effect, heartworm preventatives are necessary evils, though you should determine how necessary based on your pet's lifestyle. There is no doubt that heartworm is a dreadful disease that threatens the lives of dogs. However, the likelihood of your dog's being bitten by an infected mosquito is slim in most places, and a mosquito-repellent (or an herbal remedy such as Wormwood or Black Walnut) is much safer for your dog and will not compromise his immune system (the way heartworm preventatives will). Should you decide to use the traditional preventative "medications," you can consider giving the pill every other or third month. Since the toxins in the pill will kill the heartworms at all stages of development, the pill would be effective in killing larvae, nymphs or adults, and it takes four months for the larvae to reach the adult stage. Thus, there is no rationale to poisoning the dog's system on a monthly basis. Lastly, do not give the pill during the winter months, since there are no mosquitoes around to pass on their infection, unless you live in a tropical environment.

Life Cycle of the Heartworm

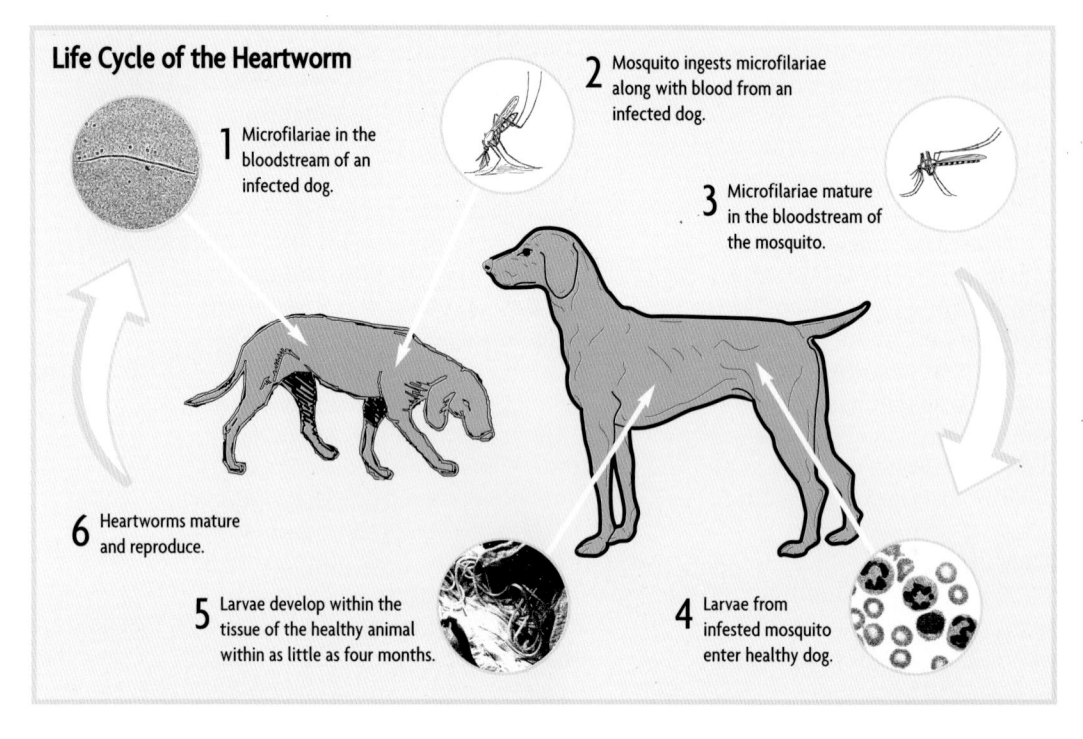

1. Microfilariae in the bloodstream of an infected dog.
2. Mosquito ingests microfilariae along with blood from an infected dog.
3. Microfilariae mature in the bloodstream of the mosquito.
4. Larvae from infested mosquito enter healthy dog.
5. Larvae develop within the tissue of the healthy animal within as little as four months.
6. Heartworms mature and reproduce.

HEARTWORMS

Heartworms are thin, extended worms up to 12 inches long, which live in a dog's heart and the major blood vessels surrounding it. Dogs may have up to 200 worms. Symptoms may be loss of energy, loss of appetite, coughing, the development of a pot belly and anemia.

Heartworms are transmitted by mosquitoes. The mosquito drinks the blood of an infected dog and takes in larvae with the blood. The larvae, called microfilariae, develop within the body of the mosquito and are passed on to the next dog bitten after the larvae mature. It takes two to three weeks for the larvae to develop to the infective stage within the body of the mosquito. Dogs are usually treated at about six weeks of age and maintained on a prophylactic dose given monthly.

Blood testing for heartworms is not necessarily indicative of how seriously your dog is infected. Although this is a dangerous disease, it is not easy for a dog to be infected. Discuss the various preventatives with your vet, as there are many different types now available. Together you can decide on a safe course of prevention for your dog.

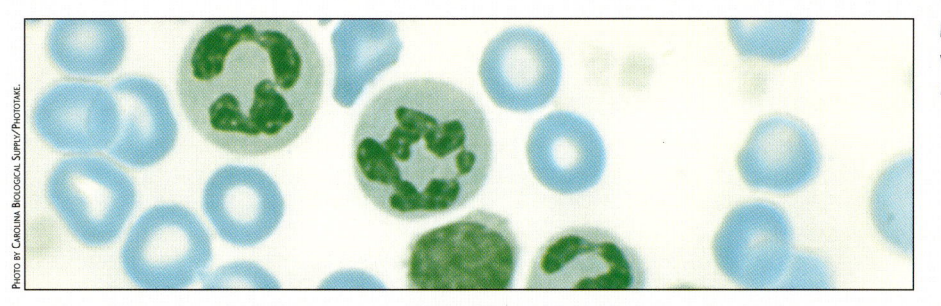

Magnified heartworm larvae, *Dirofilaria immitis.*

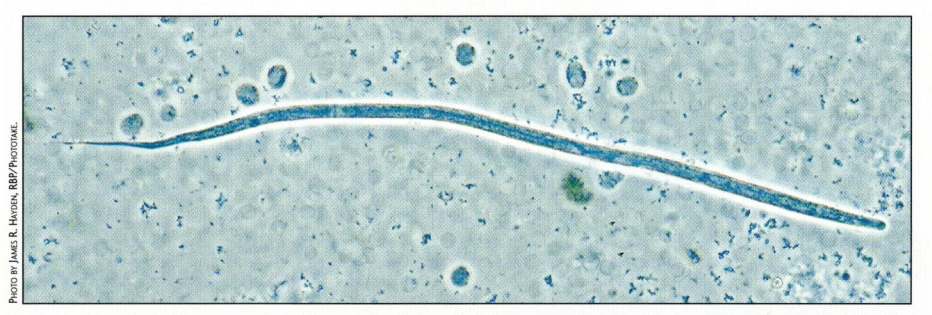

Heartworm, *Dirofilaria immitis.*

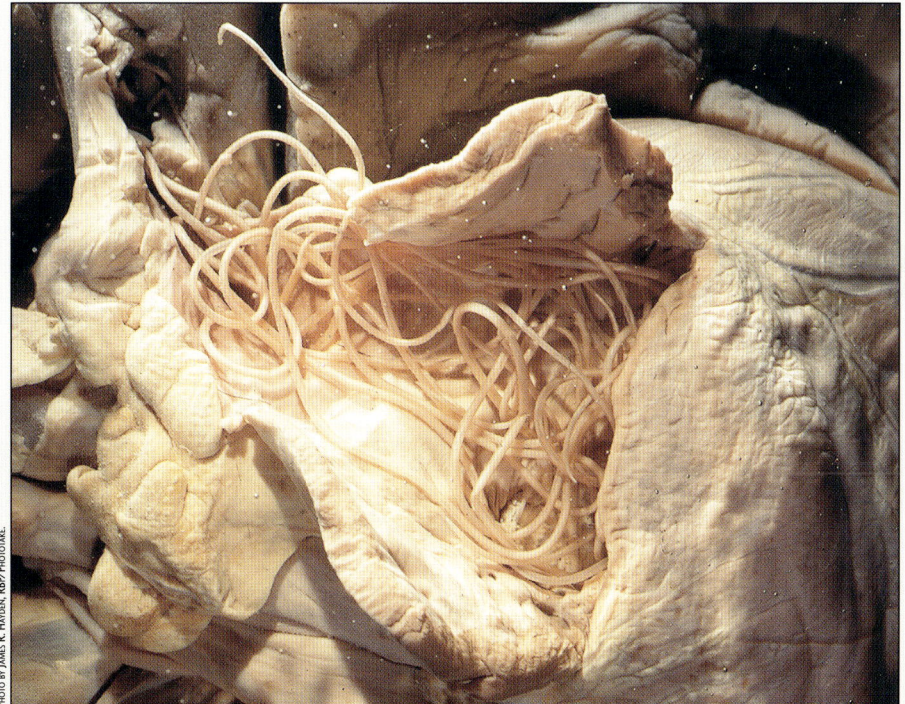

The heart of a dog infected with canine heartworm, *Dirofilaria immitis.*

HOMEOPATHY:
an alternative to conventional medicine

"Less is Most"
Using this principle, the strength of a homeopathic remedy is measured by the number of serial dilutions that were undertaken to create it. The greater the number of serial dilutions, the greater the strength of the homeopathic remedy. The potency of a remedy that has been made by making a dilution of 1 part in 100 parts (or 1/100) is 1c or 1cH. If this remedy is subjected to a series of further dilutions, each one being 1/100, a more dilute and stronger remedy is produced. If the remedy is diluted in this way six times, it is called 6c or 6cH. A dilution of 6c is 1 part in 1,000,000,000,000. In general, higher potencies in more frequent doses are better for acute symptoms and lower potencies in more infrequent doses are more useful for chronic, long-standing problems.

CURING OUR DOGS NATURALLY
Holistic medicine means treating the whole animal as a unique, perfect, living being. Generally, holistic treatments do not suppress the symptoms that the body naturally produces, as do most medications prescribed by conventional doctors and vets. Holistic methods seek to cure disease by regaining balance and harmony in the patient's environment. Some of these methods include use of nutritional therapy, herbs, flower essences, aromatherapy, acupuncture, massage, chiropractic and, of course, the most popular holistic approach, homeopathy.

Homeopathy is a theory or system of treating illness with small doses of substances which, if administered in larger quantities, would produce the symptoms that the patient already has. This approach is often described as "like cures like." Although modern veterinary medicine is geared toward the "quick fix," homeopathy relies on the belief that, given the time, the body is able to heal itself and return to its natural, healthy state.

Choosing a remedy to cure a problem in our dogs is the difficult part of homeopathy. Consult with your vet for a professional diagnosis of your dog's symptoms. Often

Health Care

these symptoms require immediate conventional care. If your vet is willing and knowledgeable, you may attempt a homeopathic remedy. Be aware that cortisone prevents homeopathic remedies from working. There are hundreds of possibilities and combinations to cure many problems in dogs, from basic physical problems such as excessive shedding, fleas or other parasites, unattractive doggy odor, bad breath, upset tummy, obesity, dry, oily or dull coat, diarrhea, ear problems or eye discharge (including tears and dry or mucousy matter), to behavioral abnormalities such as fear of loud noises, habitual licking, poor appetite, excessive barking and various phobias. From alumina to zincum metallicum, the remedies span the planet and the imagination…from flowers and weeds to chemicals, insect droppings, diesel smoke and volcanic ash.

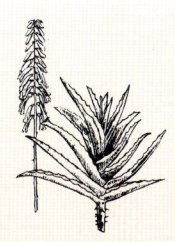

Using "Like to Treat Like"

Unlike conventional medicines that suppress symptoms, homeopathic remedies treat illnesses with small doses of substances that, if administered in larger quantities, would produce the symptoms that the patient already has. While the same homeopathic remedy can be used to treat different symptoms in different dogs, here are some interesting remedies and their uses.

Apis Mellifica
(made from honey bee venom) can be used for allergies or to reduce swelling that occurs in acutely infected kidneys.

Diesel Smoke
can be used to help control travel sickness.

Calcarea Fluorica
(made from calcium fluoride, which helps harden bone structure) can be useful in treating hard lumps in tissues.

Natrum Muriaticum
(made from common salt, sodium chloride) is useful in treating thin, thirsty dogs.

Nitricum Acidum
(made from nitric acid) is used for symptoms you would expect to see from contact with acids, such as lesions, especially where the skin joins the linings of body orifices or openings such as the lips and nostrils.

Symphytum
(made from the herb Knitbone, *Symphytum officianale*) is used to encourage bones to heal.

Urtica Urens
(made from the common stinging nettle) is used in treating painful, irritating rashes.

HOMEOPATHIC REMEDIES FOR YOUR DOG

Symptom/Ailment	Possible Remedy
ALLERGIES	Apis Mellifica 30c, Astacus Fluviatilis 6c, Pulsatilla 30c, Urtica Urens 6c
ALOPECIA	Alumina 30c, Lycopodium 30c, Sepia 30c, Thallium 6c
ANAL GLANDS (BLOCKED)	Hepar Sulphuris Calcareum 30c, Sanicula 6c, Silicea 6c
ARTHRITIS	Rhus Toxicodendron 6c, Bryonia Alba 6c
CANINE COUGH	Drosera 6c, Ipecacuanha 30c
CATARACT	Calcarea Carbonica 6c, Conium Maculatum 6c, Phosphorus 30c, Silicea 30c
CONSTIPATION	Alumina 6c, Carbo Vegetabilis 30c, Graphites 6c, Nitricum Acidum 30c, Silicea 6c
COUGHING	Aconitum Napellus 6c, Belladonna 30c, Hyoscyamus Niger 30c, Phosphorus 30c
DIARRHEA	Arsenicum Album 30c, Aconitum Napellus 6c, Chamomilla 30c, Mercurius Corrosivus 30c
DRY EYE	Zincum Metallicum 30c
EAR PROBLEMS	Aconitum Napellus 30c, Belladonna 30c, Hepar Sulphuris 30c, Tellurium 30c, Psorinum 200c
EYE PROBLEMS	Borax 6c, Aconitum Napellus 30c, Graphites 6c, Staphysagria 6c, Thuja Occidentalis 30c
GLAUCOMA	Aconitum Napellus 30c, Apis Mellifica 6c, Phosphorus 30c
HEAT STROKE	Belladonna 30c, Gelsemium Sempervirens 30c, Sulphur 30c
HICCOUGHS	Cinchona Deficinalis 6c
HIP DYSPLASIA	Colocynthis 6c, Rhus Toxicodendron 6c, Bryonia Alba 6c
INCONTINENCE	Argentum Nitricum 6c, Causticum 30c, Conium Maculatum 30c, Pulsatilla 30c, Sepia 30c
INSECT BITES	Apis Mellifica 30c, Cantharis 30c, Hypericum Perforatum 6c, Urtica Urens 30c
ITCHING	Alumina 30c, Arsenicum Album 30c, Carbo Vegetabilis 30c, Hypericum Perforatum 6c, Mezerium 6c, Sulphur 30c
MASTITIS	Apis Mellifica 30c, Belladonna 30c, Urtica Urens 1m
MOTION SICKNESS	Cocculus 6c, Petroleum 6c
PATELLAR LUXATION	Gelsemium Sempervirens 6c, Rhus Toxicodendron 6c
PENIS PROBLEMS	Aconitum Napellus 30c, Hepar Sulphuris Calcareum 30c, Pulsatilla 30c, Thuja Occidentalis 6c
PUPPY TEETHING	Calcarea Carbonica 6c, Chamomilla 6c, Phytolacca 6c

Recognizing a Sick Dog

Unlike colicky babies and cranky children, our canine kids cannot tell us when they are feeling ill. Therefore, there are a number of signs that owners can identify to know that their dogs are not feeling well.

Take note for physical manifestations such as:

- unusual, bad odor, including bad breath
- excessive shedding
- wax in the ears, chronic ear irritation
- oily, flaky, dull haircoat
- mucus, tearing or similar discharge in the eyes
- fleas or mites
- mucus in stool, diarrhea
- sensitivity to petting or handling
- licking at paws, scratching face, etc.

Keep an eye out for behavioral changes as well including:

- lethargy, idleness
- lack of patience or general irritability
- lack of interest in food
- phobias (fear of people, loud noises, etc.)
- strange behavior, suspicion, fear
- coprophagia
- more frequent barking
- whimpering, crying

Get Well Soon

You don't need a DVM to provide good TLC to your sick or recovering dog, but you do need to pay attention to some details that normally wouldn't bother him. The following tips will aid Fido's recovery and get him back on his paws again:

- Keep his space free of irritating smells, like heavy perfumes and air fresheners.
- Rest is the best medicine! Avoid harsh lighting that will prevent your dog from sleeping. Shade him from bright sunlight during the day and dim the lights in the evening.
- Keep the noise level down. Animals are more sensitive to sound when they are sick.

- Be attentive to any necessary temperature adjustments. A dog with a fever needs a cool room and cold liquids. A bitch that is whelping or recovering from surgery will be more comfortable in a warm room, consuming warm liquids and food.
- You wouldn't send a sick child back to school early, so don't rush your dog back into a full routine until he seems absolutely ready.

Number-One Killer Disease in Dogs: CANCER

In every age, there is a word associated with a disease or plague that causes humans to shudder. In the 21st century, that word is "cancer." Just as cancer is the leading cause of death in humans, it claims nearly half the lives of dogs that die from a natural disease as well as half the dogs that die over the age of ten years.

Described as a genetic disease, cancer becomes a greater risk as the dog ages. Vets and dog owners have become increasingly aware of the threat of cancer to dogs. Statistics reveal that one dog in every five will develop cancer, the most common of which is skin cancer. Many cancers, including prostate, ovarian and breast cancer, can be avoided by spaying and neutering our dogs by the age of six months.

Early detection of cancer can save or extend a dog's life, so it is absolutely vital for owners to have their dogs examined by a qualified vet or oncologist immediately upon detection of any abnormality. Certain dietary guidelines have also proven to reduce the onset and spread of cancer. Foods based on fish rather than beef, due to the presence of Omega-3 fatty acids, are recommended. Other amino acids such as glutamine have significant benefits for canines, particularly those breeds that show a greater susceptibility to cancer.

Cancer management and treatments promise hope for future generations of canines. Since the disease is genetic, breeders should never breed a dog whose parents, grandparents and any related siblings have developed cancer. It is difficult to know whether to exclude an otherwise healthy dog from a breeding program, as the disease does not manifest itself until the dog's senior years.

RECOGNIZE CANCER WARNING SIGNS

Since early detection can possibly rescue your dog from becoming a cancer statistic, it is essential for owners to recognize the possible signs and seek the assistance of a qualified professional.

- Abnormal bumps or lumps that continue to grow
- Bleeding or discharge from any body cavity
- Persistent stiffness or lameness
- Recurrent sores or sores that do not heal
- Inappetence
- Breathing difficulties
- Weight loss
- Bad breath or odors
- General malaise and fatigue
- Eating and swallowing problems
- Difficulty urinating and defecating

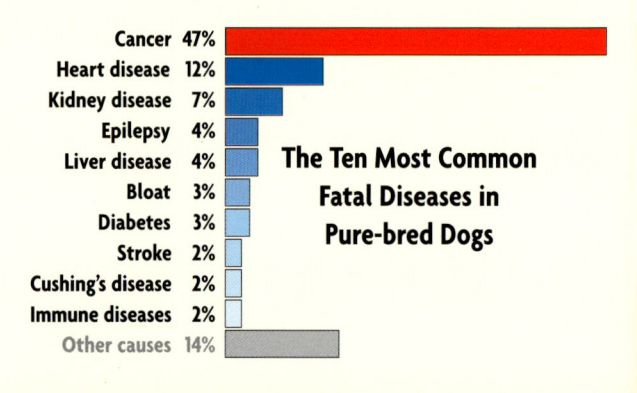

The Ten Most Common Fatal Diseases in Pure-bred Dogs

Disease	%
Cancer	47%
Heart disease	12%
Kidney disease	7%
Epilepsy	4%
Liver disease	4%
Bloat	3%
Diabetes	3%
Stroke	2%
Cushing's disease	2%
Immune diseases	2%
Other causes	14%

YOUR SENIOR
BRACCO ITALIANO

The term "old" is a qualitative term. For dogs, as well as for their masters, old is relative. Certainly we can all distinguish between a puppy Bracco Italiano and an adult Bracco Italiano—there are the obvious physical traits, such as size, appearance and facial expressions, and personality traits. Puppies and young dogs like to play with children. Children's natural exuberance is a good match for the seemingly endless energy of young dogs. They like to run, jump, chase and retrieve. When dogs grow older and cease their interaction with children, they are often thought of as being too old to keep pace with the children. On the other hand, if a Bracco is only exposed to people with quieter lifestyles, his life will normally be less active and the decrease in his activity level as he ages will not be as obvious.

If people live to be 100 years old, dogs live to be 20 years old. While this might sound like a good rule of thumb, it is very inaccurate. When trying to compare dog years to human years, you cannot make a generalization about all dogs. You can make the generalization that 12 years is a good lifespan for a Bracco. Dogs generally are considered physically mature by three years of age (or earlier), but can reproduce even earlier. So it is more accurate to estimate that the first three years of a dog's life are comparable to seven times that of humans. That means a 3-year-old dog is like a 21-year-old human. However, as the curve of comparison shows, there is no hard and fast rule for comparing dog and human ages. Small breeds tend to live longer than large breeds, some breeds' adolescent periods last longer than others' and some breeds experience rapid periods of growth. The comparison is made even more difficult, for, likewise, not all humans age at the same rate.

WHAT TO LOOK FOR IN SENIORS

Most vets and behaviorists use the seven-year mark as the time to consider a dog a "senior." This term does not imply that the dog is geriatric and has begun to fail in mind and body. Aging is essentially a slowing process. Humans readily admit that they feel a difference in their activity level from age 20 to 30, and then from 30 to 40, etc. By treating the seven-year-old dog as a senior, owners are able to implement certain therapeutic and preventative medical strategies with the help of their vets.

A senior-care program should include at least two veterinary visits per year and screening sessions to determine the dog's health status, as well as nutritional counseling. Vets determine the senior dog's health status through a blood smear for a complete blood count, serum chemistry profile with electrolytes, urinalysis, blood pressure check, electrocardiogram, ocular tonometry (pressure on the eyeball) and dental prophylaxis.

Such an extensive program for senior dogs is well advised before owners start to see the obvious physical signs of aging, such as slower and inhibited movement, graying, increased sleep/nap periods and disinterest in play and other activity. This preventative program promises a longer, healthier life for the aging dog. Other physical problems common in aging dogs are the loss of sight and hearing, arthritis, kidney and liver failure, diabetes mellitus, heart disease and Cushing's disease (a hormonal disease).

In addition to the physical manifestations discussed, there are some behavioral changes and problems related to aging dogs. Dogs suffering from hearing or vision loss, dental discomfort or arthritis can become aggressive. Likewise, the near-deaf and/or blind dog may be startled more easily and react in an unexpectedly aggressive manner. Seniors suffering from senility can become more impatient and irritable. Housesoiling accidents are associated with loss of mobility, kidney problems and loss of sphincter control as well as plaque accumulation, physiological brain changes and reactions to medications. Older dogs, just like young puppies, can suffer from separation anxiety, which can lead to excessive barking, whining, housesoiling and destructive behavior. Seniors may become fearful of everyday sounds, such as vacuum cleaners, heaters, thunder and passing traffic. Some dogs have difficulty sleeping, due to discomfort, the need for frequent toilet visits and the like.

Owners should avoid spoiling the older dog with too many treats. Obesity is a common problem in older dogs and subtracts years from their lives. Keep the senior dog as trim as possible, since excess weight puts additional stress on the body's vital organs. Some breeders recommend supplementing the diet with foods high in fiber and lower in calories. Adding fresh vegetables and marrow broth to the senior's diet makes a tasty, low-calorie, low-fat supplement. Vets also offer specialty diets for senior dogs that are worth exploring.

Your dog, as he nears his twilight years, needs your patience and good care more than ever. Never punish an older dog for an accident or abnormal behavior. For all the years of love, protection and companionship that your dog has provided, he deserves special attention and courtesies. The older dog may need to relieve himself at 3 a.m. because he can no longer hold it for eight hours. Older dogs may not be able to remain crated for more than two or three hours. It may be time to give up a sofa or chair to your old friend. Although he may not seem as enthusiastic about your attention and petting, he does appreciate the considerations you offer as he gets older.

Your Bracco Italiano does not understand why his world is slowing down. Owners must make their dogs' transition into their golden years as pleasant and rewarding as possible.

WHAT TO DO WHEN THE TIME COMES

You are never fully prepared to make a rational decision about putting your dog to sleep. It is very obvious that you love your Bracco or you would not be reading this book. Putting a beloved dog to sleep is extremely difficult. It is a decision that must be made with your vet. You are usually forced to make the decision when your dog experiences one or more life-threatening symptoms, requiring you to seek veterinary assistance.

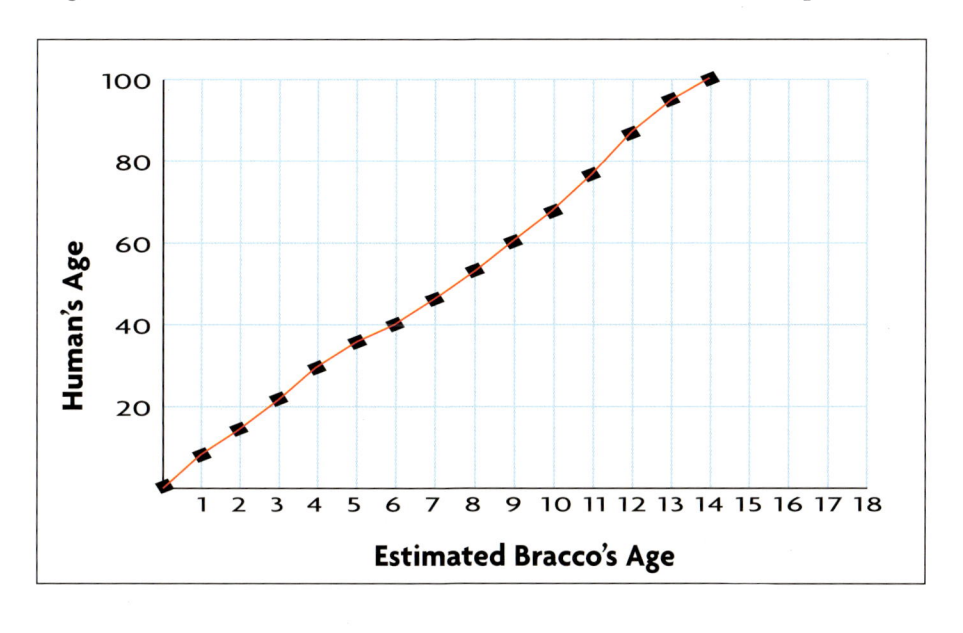

If the prognosis of the malady indicates that the end is near and that your beloved pet will only continue to suffer and experience no enjoyment for the balance of his life, then euthanasia is the right choice.

What is Euthanasia?
Euthanasia derives from the Greek, meaning "good death." In other words, it means the planned, painless killing of a dog suffering from a painful, incurable condition, or who is so aged that he cannot walk, see, eat or control his excretory functions. Euthanasia is usually accomplished by injection with an overdose of anesthesia or a barbiturate. Aside from the prick of the needle, the experience is usually painless.

Making the Decision
The decision to euthanize your dog is never easy. The days during which the dog becomes ill and the end occurs can be unusually stressful for you. If this is your first experience with the death of a loved one, you may need the comfort dictated by your religious beliefs. If you are the head of the family and have children, you should have involved them in the decision of putting your Bracco to sleep. Usually your dog can be maintained on drugs in the vet's clinic for a few days in order to give you ample time to make a decision. During this time, talking with members of your family or with people who have lived through the same experience can ease the burden of your decision.

The Final Resting Place
Dogs can have some of the same privileges as humans. The remains of your beloved dog can be buried in a pet cemetery, which is generally expensive. If your dog has died at home, he can be buried in your yard in a place suitably marked with a stone or a newly planted tree or shrub, if this is allowed where you live. Alternatively, your dog can be cremated individually and the ashes returned to you. A less expensive option is mass cremation, although, of course, the ashes cannot then be returned. Vets can usually arrange the cremation on your behalf or can help you locate a nearby pet cemetery. The cost of these options should always be discussed frankly and openly with your vet.

Getting Another Dog?
The grief of losing your beloved dog will be as lasting as the grief of losing a human friend or relative. In most cases, if your dog died of old age (if there is such a thing), he had slowed down considerably. Do you want a new Bracco Italiano puppy to replace him? Or are you better off finding a more mature Bracco, say two to three years of age, which will usually be housetrained and will have an already developed personality. In this case, you can find out if you like each other after a few hours of being together.

SHOWING YOUR
BRACCO ITALIANO

When you purchase your Bracco Italiano, you will make it clear to the breeder whether you want one just as a lovable companion and pet, or if you hope to be buying a Bracco with show prospects. No reputable breeder will sell you a young puppy and tell you that it is *definitely* of show quality, for so much can go wrong during the early months of a puppy's development. If you plan to show, what you will hopefully have acquired is a puppy with "show potential." To the novice, exhibiting a Bracco in the show ring may look easy, but it takes a lot of hard work and devotion to do top winning at a national specialty or an all-breed show, like the World Dog Show.

The first concept that the canine novice learns when watching a dog show is that each dog first competes against members of his own breed. Once the judge has selected the best member of each breed (Best of Breed), provided that the show is judged on a Group system, that chosen dog will compete with other dogs in his group. Finally, the dogs chosen first in each group will compete for Best in Show.

The second concept that you must understand is that the dogs are not actually compared against one another. The judge compares each dog against his breed standard, the written description of the ideal specimen that is approved by the hosting kennel club, such as the United Kennel Club (UKC) or the American Rare Breed Association (ARBA) in the US, or the Fédération Cynologique Internationale (FCI). While some early breed standards were indeed based on specific dogs that were famous or popular, many dedicated enthusiasts say that a perfect specimen, as described in the standard, has never walked into a show ring, has never been bred and, to the

The top three dogs at the 2000 World Dog Show, led by the Best in Show winner, a Bracco Italiano.

woe of dog breeders around the globe, does not exist. Breeders attempt to get as close to this ideal as possible with every litter, but theoretically the "perfect" dog is so elusive that it is impossible. (And if the "perfect" dog were born, breeders and judges would never agree that it was "perfect.")

If you are interested in exploring the world of dog showing, your best bet is to join your local breed club or a parent club like the North American Bracco Italiano Club. These clubs often host both regional and national specialties, shows only for Bracchi, which can include conformation as well as obedience and agility trials, field trials and hunting events. Even if you have no intention of competing with your Bracco, a specialty is like a festival for lovers of the breed who congregate to share their favorite topic: the Bracco Italiano! Clubs also send out newsletters, and some organize training days and seminars in order that people may learn more about their chosen breed.

If your Bracco is six months of age or older and registered with the hosting kennel club, you can enter him in a dog show where the breed is offered classes. Provided that your Bracco does not have a disqualifying fault, he can compete. Only unaltered dogs can be entered in a dog show, so if you have spayed or neutered your Bracco, your dog cannot compete in conformation shows. The reason for this is simple. Dog shows are the main forum to prove which representatives of a breed are worthy of being bred. Only dogs that have achieved championships—the dog world's "seal of approval" for quality in pure-bred dogs—should be bred. Altered dogs, however, can participate in other events such as obedience trials and tracking.

Before you actually step into the ring, you would be well advised to sit back and observe the judge's ring procedure. If it is your first time in the ring, stand back and study how the exhibitor in front of you is performing. The judge asks each handler to stand or "stack" the dog, hopefully showing the dog off to his best advantage. The judge will observe the dog from a distance and from different

CLUB CONTACTS

You can get information about dog shows from the national kennel clubs:

United Kennel Club
100 E. Kilgore Road, Kalamazoo, MI 49002
www.ukcdogs.com

American Rare Breed Association
9921 Frank Tippett Road
Cheltenham, MD 20623
www.arba.org

Fédération Cynologique Internationale
14, rue Leopold II, B-6530 Thuin, Belgium
www.fci.be

A group of Bracchi and their handler, awaiting their turn in the ring.

angles, and approach the dog to check his teeth, overall structure, alertness and muscle tone, as well as consider how well the dog "conforms" to the standard. Most importantly, the judge will have the exhibitor move the dog around the ring in some pattern that he should specify. Finally, the judge will give the dog one last look before moving on to the next exhibitor.

If you are not in the top four in your class at your first show, do not be discouraged. Be patient and consistent, and you may eventually find yourself in a winning line-up. Remember that the winners were once in your shoes and have devoted many hours and much money to earn the placement. If you find that your dog is losing every time and never getting a nod, it may be time to consider a different dog sport or to just enjoy your Bracco as a pet. Parent clubs offer other events, such as agility, tracking, obedience, instinct tests and more, which may be of interest to the owner of a well-trained Bracco.

OBEDIENCE TRIALS
Obedience trials in the US trace back to the early 1930s when organized obedience training was developed to demonstrate how well dog and owner could work together. The pioneer of obedience trials is Mrs. Helen Whitehouse

Walker, a Standard Poodle fancier, who designed a series of exercises after the Associated Sheep, Police Army Dog Society of Great Britain. Since the days of Mrs. Walker, obedience trials have grown by leaps and bounds, and today there are thousands of trials held in the US alone every year, with more than 100,000 dogs competing. Any registered dog can enter an obedience trial, regardless of conformational disqualifications or neutering.

AGILITY TRIALS

Agility is designed so that the handler demonstrates how well the dog can work at his side. The handler directs his dog over an obstacle course that includes jumps as well as tires, the dog walk, weave poles, pipe tunnels, collapsed tunnels, etc. While working his way through the course, the dog must keep one eye and ear on the handler and the rest of his body on the course. The handler gives verbal and hand signals to guide the dog through the course.

The first organization to promote agility trials in the US was the United States Dog Agility Association, Inc. (USDAA), which was established in 1986 and spawned numerous member clubs around the country. Three titles are available through the USDAA: Agility Dog (AD), Advanced Agility Dog (AAD) and Master Agility Dog (MAD).

Agility is great fun for dog and owner with many rewards for everyone involved. Interested owners should join a training club that has obstacles and experienced agility handlers who can introduce you and your dog to the "ropes" (and tires, tunnels, etc.). Bracchi also can compete and earn titles in agility trials held by the UKC. Dogs typically must be 12 months of age or older to compete in agility, as this type of exercise is not recommended for developing puppies.

TRACKING

Any dog is capable of tracking, using his nose to follow a trail. Tracking tests are exciting and competitive ways to test your Bracco's keen scenting ability, and his ability to search and rescue. Tracking is used throughout the world by the police and by military establishments, for a dog's scenting ability can be an invaluable asset when trying to trace people for various reasons.

Tracking tests involves the

TEMPERAMENT PLUS
Although it seems that physical conformation is the only factor considered in the show ring, temperament is also of utmost importance. An aggressive or fearful dog should not be shown, as bad behavior will not be tolerated and may pose a threat to the judge, other exhibitors, you and your dog.

Showing

> **NEATNESS COUNTS**
> Surely you've spent hours grooming your dog to perfection for the show ring, but don't forget about yourself! While the dog should be the center of attention, it is important that you also appear neat and clean. Wear smart, appropriate clothes and comfortable shoes in a color that contrasts with your dog's coat. Look and act like a professional.

dogs' picking up and following a human scent, over courses with directional changes and different types of terrain. Wearing a harness, to which a long tracking line is attached, the handler works the dog. Because of the length of line attached, the handler does not interfere with the dog unduly while tracking. This is also an aid to the handler in keeping up with the dog's pace; if there were no harness, the dog's speed would in most cases be too great for humans to manage.

In some tracking events, a dog is expected to recover articles placed along the track. The dog is not present when the track is laid, nor is the handler, and a track can be up to three hours old before being worked. Tracking is demanding work, and various titles can be earned based on the difficulty of the course, with each progressive title requiring completion of a more complex course. Weather and terrain both play important roles in the likelihood of success. Bracchi used for tracking need to be in good condition, as indeed do their handlers.

FIELD TRIALS AND HUNTING EVENTS

The rules and regulations of field and hunting events vary according to the country in which they are held, and also according to the hosting club. Contact a breed club, national kennel club or specialty hunting club to find out about events in your area and how to become involved with your Bracco. In the US, the Bracco competes in hunting events run by the UKC and the North American Versatile Hunting Dog Association, the latter is strictly a hunting organization. These performance events are natural competitive venues for the breed, as they test the very skills for which the Bracco was bred. Remember that the Bracco Italiano is an HPR breed, and is thus amply qualified to participate in many aspects of field work and hunting.

The Bracco ranks as one of the world's most talented HPR field dogs.

BEHAVIOR OF YOUR BRACCO ITALIANO

As a Bracco Italiano owner, you have selected your dog so that you and your loved ones can have a companion, a protector, a friend and a four-legged family member. You invest time, money and effort to care for and train the family's new charge. Of course, this chosen canine behaves perfectly! Well, perfectly like a *dog*.

THINK LIKE A DOG
Dogs do not think like humans, nor do humans think like dogs, though we try. Unfortunately, a dog is incapable of comprehending how humans think, so the responsibility falls on the owner to adopt a viable canine mindset. Dogs cannot rationalize, and dogs exist in the present moment. Many a dog owner makes the mistake in training of thinking that he can reprimand his dog for something the dog did a while ago. Basically, you cannot even reprimand a dog for something he did 20 seconds ago! Either catch him in the act or forget it! It is a waste of your and your dog's time—in his mind, you are reprimanding him for whatever he is doing at that moment.

The following behavioral problems represent some which owners most commonly encounter. Every dog is unique and every situation is unique. No author could purport for you to solve your Bracco's problems simply by reading a chapter in a book. Here we outline some basic "dogspeak" so that owners' chances of solving behavioral problems are increased. Discuss bad habits with your vet and he can recommend a behavioral specialist to consult in appropriate cases. Since behavioral abnormalities are the main reason for owners' abandoning their pets, we hope that you will make a valiant effort to solve your Bracco's problems. Patience and understanding are virtues that must dwell in every pet-loving household.

SEPARATION ANXIETY
Recognized by behaviorists as the most common form of stress for dogs, separation anxiety can also lead to destructive behaviors in your dog. It's more than your Bracco's howling his displeasure at your leaving the house and his being left alone. This is a normal reaction, no different than the child who cries as his mother leaves him on the first day at school. Separation anxiety is more serious.

In fact, if you are constantly with your dog, he will come to expect you with him all of the time, making it even more traumatic for him when you are not there.

Obviously, you enjoy spending time with your dog, and he thrives on your love and attention. However, it should not become a dependent relationship in which he is heartbroken without you. This broken heart can also bring on destructive behavior as well as loss of appetite, depression and lack of interest in play and interaction. Canine behaviorists have been spending much time and energy to help owners better understand the significance of this stressful condition.

One thing you can do to minimize separation anxiety is to make your entrances and exits as low-key as possible. Do not give your dog a long drawn-out goodbye, and do not lavish him with hugs and kisses when you return. This is giving in to the attention that he craves, and it will only make him miss it more when you are away. Another thing you can try is to give your dog a treat when you leave; this will not only keep him occupied and keep his mind off the fact that you have just left, but it will also help him associate your leaving with a pleasant experience.

You may have to accustom your dog to being left alone at intervals. Of course, when your dog starts whimpering as you

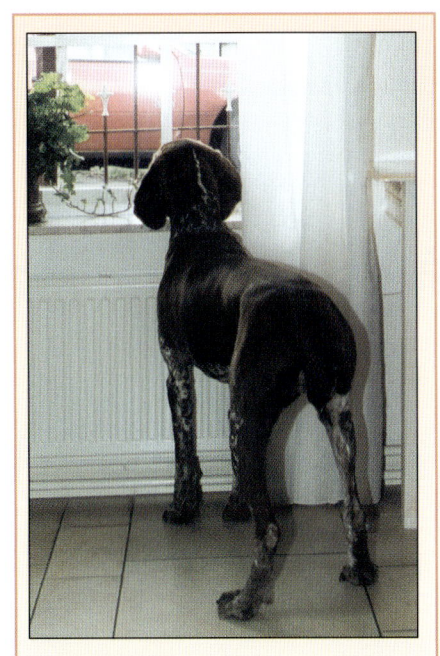

I'M HOME!
Dogs left alone for varying lengths of time may often react wildly when their owners return. Sometimes they run, jump, bite, chew, tear things apart, wet themselves, gobble their food or behave in very undisciplined ways. If your dog behaves in this manner upon your return home, allow him to calm down before greeting him or he will consider your attention as a reward for his antics.

approach the door, your first instinct will be to run to him and comfort him, but do not do it! Eventually he will adjust to your absence. His anxiety stems from being placed in an unfamiliar situation; by familiarizing him with being alone, he will learn that he will survive. That is not to say you should purposely leave your dog home alone, but the dog needs to know that, while he can depend on you for his care, you do not have to be by his side 24 hours a day. Some behaviorists recommend tiring the dog out before you leave home—take him for a good long walk or engage in a game of fetch in the backyard.

When the dog is alone in the house, he should be placed in his crate—another distinct advantage to crate-training your dog. The crate should be placed in his familiar happy family area, where he normally sleeps and already feels comfortable, thereby making him feel more at ease when he is alone. Be sure to give the dog a special chew toy to enjoy while he settles into his crate.

"Are you home yet?" Owners that are away during the day should spend time with their dogs whenever they are home and make sure to include their dogs as a part of family life.

AGGRESSION

Although the Bracco is not a breed known for aggressive tendencies, this is still an issue that concerns all responsible dog owners. Aggression can be a very big problem in dogs, and, when not controlled, always becomes dangerous. An aggressive dog, no matter the size, may lunge at, bite or even attack a person or another dog. Aggressive behavior is not to be tolerated. It is more than just inappropriate behavior; it is painful for a family to watch their dog become unpredictable in his behavior to the point where they are afraid of him. While not all aggressive behavior is dangerous, things like growling, baring teeth, etc., can be frightening. It is important to ascertain why the dog is acting in this manner. Aggression is a display of dominance, and the dog should not have the dominant role in his pack, which is, in this case, your family.

It is important not to challenge an aggressive dog, as this could provoke an attack. Observe your Bracco's body language. Does he make direct eye contact and stare? Does he try to make himself as large as possible: ears pricked, chest out, tail erect? Height and size signify authority in a dog pack—being taller or "above" another dog literally means that he is "above" in social status. These body signals tell you that your Bracco thinks he is in charge, a problem that needs to be addressed. An aggressive dog is unpredictable; you never know when he is going to strike and what he is going to do. You cannot understand why a dog that is playful one minute is growling the next.

Fear is a common cause of aggression in dogs. Perhaps your Bracco had a negative experience as a puppy, which causes him to be fearful when a similar situation presents itself later in life. The dog may act aggressively in order to protect himself from whatever is making him afraid. It is not always easy to determine what is making your dog fearful, but if you can isolate what brings out the fear reaction, you can help the dog get over it.

Supervise your Bracco's interactions with people and other dogs, and praise the dog when it goes well. If he starts to act aggressively in a situation, correct him and remove him from the situation. Do not let people approach the dog and start petting him without your express permission. That way, you can have the dog sit to accept petting, and praise him when he behaves properly. You are focusing on praise and on modifying his behavior by rewarding him when he acts appropriately. By being gentle and by supervising his interactions, you are showing him that there is no need to be afraid or defensive.

The best solution is to consult a behavioral specialist to help you pinpoint the cause of your dog's aggression and do something about it. An aggressive dog cannot be trusted, and a dog that cannot be trusted is not safe to have as a family pet. If, very unusually, you find that your pet has become untrustworthy and you feel it necessary to seek a new home with a more suitable family and environment, explain fully to the new owners all of your reasons for rehoming the dog to be fair to all concerned.

NO BUTTS ABOUT IT!
Dogs get to know each other by sniffing each other's backsides. It seems that each dog has a telltale odor, probably created by the anal glands. It also distinguishes sex and signals when a female will be receptive to a male's attention. Some dogs snap at another dog's intrusion of their private parts.

A little roughhousing among dogs is harmless, and is natural dog behavior, although it may look otherwise to their owners.

Aggression toward Other Dogs

The Bracco also is not known to be especially dog-aggressive. Typically, a dog's aggressive behavior toward another dog stems from not enough exposure to other dogs at an early age. If in the unusual case that other dogs make your Bracco nervous and agitated, he will lash out as a protective mechanism. A dog that has not received sufficient exposure to other canines tends to think that he is the only dog on the planet. The animal becomes so dominant that he does not even show signs that he is fearful or threatened. Without growling or any other physical signal as a warning, he will lunge at and bite the other dog.

A way to correct this is to let your Bracco approach another dog when walking on lead. Watch very closely and, at the first sign of aggression, correct your Bracco and pull him away. Scold him for any sign of discomfort, and then praise him when he ignores the other dog. Keep this up until either he stops the aggressive behavior, learns to ignore other dogs or even accepts other dogs. Praise him lavishly for his correct behavior.

Dominant Aggression

A social hierarchy is firmly established in a wild dog pack. The dog wants to dominate those under him and please those above him. Dogs know that there must be a leader. If you are not the obvious choice for emperor, the dog will assume the throne! In training a dog to obey commands, the owner is reinforcing that he is the "top dog" in the pack.

An important part of training is taking every opportunity to reinforce that you are the leader. The simple action of making your Bracco sit to wait for his food instead of allowing him to run up to get it when he wants it says that you control when he eats; he is dependent on you for food. Although it may be difficult, do not give in to your dog's wishes every time he whines at you or looks at you with pleading eyes. It is a constant effort to show the dog that his place in the pack is at the bottom.

This is not meant to sound inhumane. You love your Bracco and you should treat him with care and affection. Dog training is not about being cruel, it is about molding the dog's behavior into what is acceptable and teaching him to live by your rules. In theory, it is quite simple: catch him in appropriate behavior and reward him for it.

With a dominant dog, punishment and negative reinforcement can have the opposite effect of what you are after. It can make a dog fearful and/or act out aggressively if he feels he is being challenged. Remember, a dominant dog perceives himself at the top of the social heap and will fight to defend his perceived status. The best way to prevent that is to never give him reason to think that he is in control in the first place.

If you are having trouble training your Bracco and it seems as if he is constantly challenging your authority, seek the help of an obedience trainer or behavioral specialist. A professional will work with both you and your dog to teach you effective techniques to use at home. Beware of trainers who rely on excessively harsh methods; scolding is necessary now and then, but the focus in your training should *always* be on positive reinforcement. The Bracco does not respond to harsh methods; this is not the way to accomplish anything with this sensitive breed.

SEXUAL BEHAVIOR

Dogs exhibit certain sexual behaviors that may have influenced your choice of male or female when you first purchased your Bracco. To a certain extent, spaying/neutering will eliminate these behaviors, but if you are purchasing a dog that you wish to breed from, you should be aware of what you will have to deal with throughout the dog's life.

Female dogs usually have two estruses per year, with each season lasting about three weeks. These are the only times in which a female dog will mate, and she usually will not allow this until the second week of the cycle, although this varies from bitch to bitch. If not bred during the heat cycle, it is not uncommon for a bitch to experience a false pregnancy, in which her mammary glands swell and she exhibits maternal tendencies toward toys or other objects.

With male dogs, owners must be aware that whole dogs (dogs who are not neutered) have the natural inclination to mark their territory. Males mark their territory by spraying small amounts of urine as they lift their legs in a macho ritual. Marking can occur both outdoors in the yard and around the neighborhood as well as indoors on furniture legs, curtains and the sofa. Such behavior can be very frustrating for the owner; early training is strongly urged before the "urge" strikes your dog. Neutering the male at an appropriate early age can solve this problem before it becomes a habit.

Other problems associated with males are wandering and mounting. Both of these habits, of course, belong to the unneutered dog, whose sexual drive leads him away from home in search of the bitch in heat. Males will mount females in heat, as well as any other dog, male or female, that happens to catch their fancy. Other possible mounting partners include his owner, the furniture, guests to the home and strangers on the street. Discourage such behavior early on. Owners must further recognize that mounting is not merely a sexual expression but also one of dominance, seen in males and females alike.

CHEWING
The national canine pastime is chewing! Every dog loves to sink his "canines" into a tasty bone, so it is important to provide your dog with appropriate chew toys so that he doesn't destroy your possessions or make a habit of gnawing on your hands and fingers. Dogs need to chew to massage their gums, to make their new teeth feel better and to exercise their jaws. This is a natural behavior that is deeply embedded in all things canine.

A comfortable spot to lie down and toys to sink his teeth into...what more could a dog ask for?

Our role as owners is not to stop the dog's chewing, but rather to redirect it to positive, chew-worthy objects. Be an informed owner and purchase proper chew toys, like strong nylon bones, that will not splinter. Be sure that the objects are safe and durable, since your dog's safety is at risk. Again, the owner is responsible for ensuring a dog-proof environment.

The best answer is prevention; that is, put your shoes, handbags and other tasty objects in their proper places (out of the reach of the growing canine mouth). Direct your puppy to his toys whenever you see him "tasting" the furniture legs or the leg of your pants. Make a loud noise to attract the pup's attention and immediately escort him to his chew toy and engage him with the toy for at least four minutes, praising and encouraging him all the while. An array of safe, interesting chew toys will keep your dog's mind and teeth occupied, and distracted from chewing on things he shouldn't.

Some trainers recommend deterrents, such as hot pepper, a bitter spice or a product designed for this purpose, to discourage the dog from chewing unwanted objects. Test these products to see which works best before investing in large quantities.

JUMPING UP
Jumping up is a dog's friendly way of saying hello! Some dog owners

do not mind when their dog jumps up. The problem arises when guests come to the house and the dog greets them in the same manner—whether they like it or not! However friendly the greeting may be, chances are that your visitors will not appreciate such enthusiasm from a large dog like your Bracco. The dog will not be able to distinguish upon whom he can jump and whom he cannot. Therefore, it is probably best to discourage this behavior entirely.

Pick a command such as "Off" (avoid using "Down" since you will use that for the dog to lie down) and tell him "Off" when he jumps up. Place him on the ground on all fours and have him sit, praising him the whole time. Always lavish him with praise and petting when he is in the sit position. In this way, you can give him a warm affectionate greeting, let him know that you are as pleased to see him as he is to see you and instill good manners at the same time!

DIGGING

Digging, which is seen as a destructive behavior to humans, is actually quite a natural behavior in dogs. Although terriers (the "earth dogs") are most associated with digging, any dog's desire to dig can be irrepressible and most frustrating to his owners. When digging occurs in your yard, it is actually a normal behavior redirected into something the dog can do in his everyday life. In the wild, a dog would be actively seeking food, making his own shelter, etc. He would be using his paws in a purposeful manner for his survival. Since you provide him with food and shelter, he has no need to use his paws for these purposes, and so the energy that he would be using may manifest itself in the form of little holes all over your lawn and flowerbeds.

Perhaps your dog is digging as a reaction to boredom—it is somewhat similar to someone eating a whole bag of chips in front of the TV—because they are there and there is nothing better to do! Basically, the answer is to provide the dog with adequate play and exercise so that his mind and paws are occupied, and so that he feels as if he is doing something useful.

Of course, digging is easiest to control if it is stopped as soon as possible, but it is often hard to catch a dog in the act. If your dog is a compulsive digger and is not easily distracted by other activities, you can designate an area on your

Although not an "earth dog" breed, some Bracchi can't resist the urge to get their paws dirty.

property where he is allowed to dig. If you catch him digging in an off-limits area of the yard, immediately take him to the approved area and praise him for digging there. Keep a close eye on him so that you can catch him in the act—that is the only way to make him understand what is permitted and what is not. If you take him to a hole he dug an hour ago and tell him "No," he will understand that you are not fond of holes, dirt or flowers. If you catch him while he is stifle-deep in your tulips, that is when he will get your message.

BARKING
Dogs cannot talk—oh, what they would say if they could! Instead, barking is a dog's way of "talking." It can be somewhat frustrating because it is not always easy to tell what a dog means by his bark—is he excited, happy, frightened or angry? Whatever it is that the dog is trying to say, he should not be punished for barking. It is only when the barking becomes excessive, and when the excessive barking becomes a bad habit, that the behavior needs to be modified.

Fortunately, Bracchi are not unduly vocal, but they will give a warning of approaching strangers. If an intruder came into your home in the middle of the night and your Bracco barked a warning, wouldn't you be pleased? You would probably deem your dog a hero, a wonderful guardian and protector of the home. On the other hand, if a friend drops by unexpectedly, rings the doorbell and is greeted with a sudden sharp bark, you would probably be annoyed at the dog. But in reality, isn't this just the same behavior? The dog does not know any better. Unless he sees who is at the door and it is someone he knows, he will bark as a means of vocalizing that his (and your) territory is being threatened. While your friend is not posing a threat, it is all the same to the dog. Barking is his means of letting you know that there is an intrusion, whether friend or foe, on your property. This type of barking is instinctive and should not be discouraged.

Excessive habitual barking, however, is a problem that should be corrected early on. As your Bracco grows up, you will be able to tell when his barking is purposeful and when it is for no reason. You will become able to distinguish your dog's different barks and

> **BARKING STANCE**
> Did you know that a dog is less likely to bark when sitting than standing? Watch your dog the next time that you suspect he is about to start barking. You'll notice that as he does, he gets up on all four feet. Hence, when teaching a dog to stop barking, it helps to get him to sit before you command him to be quiet.

their meanings. For example, the bark when someone comes to the door will be different than the bark when he is excited to see you. It is similar to a person's tone of voice, except that the dog has to rely totally on tone of voice because he does not have the benefit of using words. An incessant barker will be evident at an early age.

There are some things that encourage a dog to bark. For example, if your dog barks non-stop for a few minutes and you give him a treat to quiet him, he believes that you are rewarding him for barking. He will associate barking with getting a treat and will keep doing it until he is rewarded. On the other hand, if you give him a command such as "Quiet" and praise him after he has stopped barking for a few seconds, he will get the idea that being "quiet" is what you want him to do.

FOOD STEALING

Is your dog devising ways of stealing food from your coffee table or kitchen counter? If so, you must answer the following questions: Is your Bracco a bit hungry, or is he "constantly famished" like many dogs seem to be? Face it, some dogs are more food-motivated than others. They are totally obsessed by the smell of food and can only think of their next meal. Food stealing is terrific fun and always yields a great reward—*food*, glorious food.

Your goal as an owner, therefore, is to be sensible about where food is placed in the home and to reprimand your dog whenever he is caught in the act of stealing. But remember, only reprimand your dog if you actually see him stealing, not later when the crime is discovered; that will be of no use at all and will only confuse him.

BEGGING

Just like food stealing, begging is a favorite pastime of hungry puppies! It achieves that same great result—*food!* Dogs quickly learn that their owners keep the "good food" for ourselves, and that we humans do not dine on dry food alone. Begging is a conditioned response related to a specific stimulus, time and place. The sounds of the kitchen, cans and bottles opening, crinkling bags, the smell of food in preparation, etc., will excite the dog, and soon the paws will be in the air!

Here is the solution to stopping this behavior: Never give in to a beggar! You are rewarding the dog for sitting pretty, jumping up, whining and rubbing his nose into you by giving him food. By ignoring the dog, you will (eventually) force the behavior into extinction. Note that the behavior is likely to get worse before it disappears, so be sure there are not any "softies" in the family who will give in to little "Oliver" every time he whimpers, "More, please."

INDEX

*Page numbers in **boldface** indicate illustrations.*

Acral lick granuloma 114
Activities 16, 18, 143
Adult diet 62
Advanced Agility Dog 144
Aggression 54, 148
—dominant 150
—toward other dogs 150
Agility 143-144
Agility Dog 144
Aging 111, 137
—signs of 138
Air travel 76
Allergy 112, 116
—airborne 114
—food 115
—parasite bite 114
American dog tick 122
American Kennel Club 15
American Rare Breed Association 15, 141, 142
Ancylostoma caninum 127
ARBA 15, 141, 142
Ascaris lumbricoides **126**
Auto-immune illness 114
Axelrod, Dr. Herbert R. 125
Barking 154
Basset Hound 15
Bathing 67
Bedding 53, 58
Begging 155
Behavioral problems 53, 56, 148-155
Behavioral specialist 146, 149, 151
Best in Show 141
Best of Breed 141
Bite 39
Bloat 24, 48, 59, 65, 116-117
Bloodhound 15
Boarding 77
Body 19
Body language 148
Bones 46, 152
Booster immunizations 109

Boredom 153
Borrelia burgdorferi 123
Bowls 48
Bracco Italiano Society 16
Breed club 37, 142
—events 143
Breed standard 26, 141
Breeder 26, 142
—finding a 39
—selection 37-38
Brown dog tick **125**
Brushing 66
Burial 140
Cancer 136
Canine cough 109-111
Car travel 74
Chew toys 45, 148, 152
Chewing 50, 57-58, 152
Cheyletiellosis mite 124
Chocolate 56
Climbing 51
Coat 21
Collar 46, 48
Color 10, 21
Colostrum 61
Commands 93-100, 153, 155
Companion dog 17-18
Coronavirus 109, 111
Crate 43, 57, 75-76, 148
Cremation 140
Crying 53, 57
Ctenocephalides **120**
Ctenocephalides canis **118**
Deer tick **123**
Delor de Ferrabouc, Ferndinando 10
Demodex mite 123
Dental care 72, 107, 109-111
Dermacentor variabilis **122-123**
Dermanyssus gallinae 125
Destructive behavior 54, 138, 146, 152

Dewclaws 19
Diet 22, 59-63, 115, 138
—adult 62
—puppy 60-61
—senior 63, 111, 138
Digging 51, 153
Dipylidium caninum 128
Dirofilaria immitis **131**
Distemper 109, 111
Dominance 55, 148, 150, 152
Ear 19
—care 69
—mite infestation 69, 125
Echinococcus multilocularis 128
Egyptian Hound 9
Elbow dysplasia 24
ENCI 10
Energy level 19
Estrus 151
Euthanasia 140
Eutrombicula alfreddugesi 125
Exercise 17-19, 59, 65
External parasites 118-125
Eyes 24
Family dog 17-18
Family introduction to pup 51
Fear 54, 138, 149
Fédération Cynologique Internationale 26, 28-29, 141
—address 142
—breed standard 26
Feeding 22, 59, 115
Feet 19
Fence 50
Field trials 145
First aid 113
First night home 52
Flea **118**, 119, **120-121**, 122, 128
—life cycle 119-120, **121**

Food 22, 59, 60
—allergies 115
—bowls 48
—fresh 60
—intolerance 116
—preference 60
—proper diet 59
—stealing 155
Gait 21
Gastric dilatation 24, 48, 116
Gastric torsion 24, 48, 116
Gender differences 39
Gonzaga family 9
Grooming 22, 66
Growth 22
Gundog 15
—breeds 10
Handling 142
Head 19
Heart problems 25
Heartworm 109, 129, **130-131**
Heat exhaustion 25
Height 21, 39
Hepatitis 109, 111
Hereditary problems 22, 25, 112
Hip dysplasia 22, 109
Home preparation for pup 42
Homeopathy 132-134
Hookworm **127**
Hounds 10
—resemblance 19
HPR 9-10
Hunt, Point and Retrieve 9
Hunting ability 10, 12, 19
Hunting events 145
Hunting method 12
Identification 77-78
IGR 120, 122
Import register 16
Insect Growth Regulator 120, 122

Insurance 40
Intelligence 17-18
Internal parasites 125-130
Italian Kennel Club 10
Italian Spinone 9-10, **12**
Italy 9, 13
Judge 26, 142
Jumping 51, 152
Kennel Club, The 16
Lead 46
Leptospirosis 109, 111
Lice **124**
Life expectancy 137
Litter size 37
Lombardy type 10
Loyalty 18
Lupus 115
Mange mite **124**
Marking territory 151
Master Agility Dog 144
Maturity 62
Medici family 9
Middle Ages 9
Milk 61
Mite 123
Molossus 9
Mounting 151-152
Movement 19, 21
Mulch 56
Nail clipping 72
Negative reinforcement 151
Neutering 105, 109-110
Nipping 56
North America 15
North American Bracco Italiano Club 15, 37
North American Versatile Hunting Dog Association 15, 145
Obedience 143
—trials 142-143
Obesity 24, 59, 63, 66, 138
Off 153
Origins of breed 9

Osteoarthritis 22, 115
Otodectes cynotis 125
Owner suitability 17
Ownership 40
Parainfluenza 109
Parasite 118-130
—bite 114
—external 118-125
—internal 125-130
Parvovirus 109, 111
Pastrone standard 13
Personality 18
Physical characteristics 18
Piedmont type 10
Pointer 10
Pointing methods 12
Pollen allergy 114
Popularity 13
Positive reinforcement 18, 149, 151
Preventative medicine 107
Proportions 21
Protein 59
Psoroptes bovi **124**
Punishment 151
Puppy
—appearance 36
—diet 60-61
—first night home 52
—growth 22
—health 38
—introduction to family 51
—personality 38, 40
—preparing home for 42
—problems 53, 56
—selection 36, 37, 40
—training 41
Puppy-proofing 49
Quiet 155
Rabies 109, 111
Rawhide 46
Renaissance period 9
Revival of breed 10
Rhabditis **126**

Rhipicephalus sanguineus **125**
Roundworm **126**
SABI 12
Safety 43, 49-50
—harness 75
Sarcoptes mite 124
Seasonal cycles 151
Segugio Italiano **11**
Senior 137
—care of 138
—diet 63, 111, 138
Sensitive nature 18
Separation anxiety 57, 138, 146
Sexual behavior 151
Shaw, Jonathan and Liz 15
Show potential 141
Size 21, 39
Skin 21
—inherited 112
—problems 111
Socialization 53, 55
Società Amatori Bracco Italiano 12
Spaying 105, 110
Spinone, Italiano 9-10, **12**
Standard 26, 141
—early 10
—first ENCI 10
Stealing food 155
Swimming 19
Tail 19
Tapeworm **128**
Teeth 107, 111
Temperament 18, 25, 107
Thebromine 56
Threadworm 129
Tick 122-**123**
Tooth care 72
Toxocara canis 126
Toys 45, 58, 152
Tracheobronchitis 110
Tracking 142-144
Training 17-18, 55
—puppy 41
Traveling 43, 74, 76

Trichuris vulpis 128
Type
—differences in 10
United Kennel Club 15, 141
—address 142
United Kingdom 15
United States 15
United States Dog Agility Association 144
Vacations 77
Vaccinations 51, 54, 105, 109
Veterinarian 51, 105, 109, 111, 125, 137
—insurance 40
—specialist 114
Walker, Mrs. Helen Whitehouse 143
Wandering 151
Water 65
—bowls 48
Weaning 62, 107
Weight 21
Whining 53, 57
Whipworm 128-129
With cats 17
With children 55
With strangers 18
Working ability 10, 12, 16, 18
Working methods 12
Working Standard 13
Worming 109
Zerbo 16

My Bracco Italiano

PUT YOUR PUPPY'S FIRST PICTURE HERE

Dog's Name _____

Date _____ Photographer _____